Gwendolyn MacEwen

VOLUME ONE

The Early Years

Gwendolyn MacEwen

VOLUME ONE
The Early Years

Edited by Margaret Atwood
and Barry Callaghan

Introduction and Introductory Notes
by Margaret Atwood

Exile Editions
1993

This edition is published by Exile Editions Limited,
20 Dale Avenue, Toronto, Ontario, Canada   M4W 1K4

SALES DISTRIBUTION:
McArthur & Company
c/o Harper Collins
1995 Markham Road
Toronto, ON
M1B 5M8
toll free:
1 800 387 0117
1 800 668 5788 (fax)

Layout and Design by MICHAEL P. CALLAGHAN
Composed and Typeset at MOONS OF JUPITER, Toronto
Photographs by JOHN MCCOMBE REYNOLDS
Printed and Bound by MARC VEILLEUX IMPRIMEUR, Quebec

The editors acknowledge, with appreciation,
the textual changes made to the "Adam's Alphabet" section
as suggested by Dorothy Shostak.

The publisher wishes to acknowledge
the assistance toward publication of the Canada Council
and the Ontario Arts Council.

The Canada Council
Conseil des Arts du Canada

ISBN 1-55096-543-3

INTRODUCTION: *THE EARLY YEARS*

For we are great statements in our days
And on the basis of that we can expect small audiences.

Gwendolyn MacEwen was born in Toronto in September 1941, during the darkest days of World War II. She died, unexpectedly and far too young, in 1987, at the age of forty-five.

Due to family disruptions — her mother was frequently hospitalized for mental illness, her father became an alcoholic — her childhood was stressful; but the conviction that she would be a poet came to her as a saving grace in early adolescence. She began publishing poetry in the well-respected journal *The Canadian Forum* when she was sixteen, and at the age of eighteen — although warned against such a rash step by more practical heads — she left high school to pursue her vocation.

The late fifties was not the best time for such a move, especially if you were a woman. In the world of conventional North American popular culture, Doris Day and Betty Crocker ruled supreme and Mom-and-Dad domesticity was the norm; rebellion against the bourgeoisie was embodied by Marlon Brando and his all-boy *Wild Ones* motorbike gang. The music was rock n' roll or jazz, heavily male both. "Artist" meant male painter; any woman rash enough to take brush in hand was regarded as a dabbler. The Beat Generation writers had a place for women, true, but only as complaisant helpmeets; they were expected to keep on cookin' and smilin' and payin' the rent, and to keep out of the hair of their genius men. Women artists of any kind, in that still heavily-Freudian era, were assumed to have adjustment problems. *Man Does, Woman Is,* as Robert Graves so dauntingly put it; and if women insisted on doing rather than being, they were likely to end up with their heads in the oven.

For Gwendolyn MacEwen, all of this was compounded you would think by location. Toronto was not exactly a centre of cosmopolitan artistic energy at the time. Montreal was considered to be the cultural heartland, for both English-speaking and French-speaking artists alike, whereas Toronto was thought of as a puritanical provincial backwater, a boring, constipated place where you couldn't get wine with dinner. Persons of taste sneered at it, even and especially those who lived there. Colonialism lingered on, and it was assumed that first-rate cultural products were imported from abroad — from Europe if you were old-fashioned, from New York if you thought of yourself as the cutting edge.

But for young writers, even young female writers, there were compensations. Cultural trends are never as oppressively homogeneous in the outbacks as they are in the centres, and in Canada there was a generation of woman poets just before MacEwen's who hadn't heard yet that they were supposed to just be: Phyllis Webb, Anne Wilkinson, Jay Macpherson, P.K. Page, Margaret Avison. And the writing community was so small, beleaguered, and desirous of reinforcements that it was welcoming to any newcomer with talent, especially such an outstanding talent as MacEwen's. Oddly enough, this period — so forbidding and desert-like to the casual view — was, for writing, an age of youthful successes. In addition to Leonard Cohen it produced Daryl Hine, who published his first major collection when he was under twenty; James Reaney, the boy wonder from Stratford; Marie-Claire Blais, the girl wonder from Quebec; Jay Macpherson, who won the country's foremost literary award when she was twenty-seven; Michael Ondaatje, b.p. nichol, Joe Rosenblatt, bill bissett —

all early publishers; and many others. So although Gwendolyn MacEwen started publishing very early, she wasn't alone.

Nor was it unusual for her to begin with poetry. Like many of her contemporaries, she eventually produced several novels and collections of short stories, and during the course of her career she also produced radio plays, translations for the theatre, and travel writing; but the poetry appeared first. Indeed, for most of the sixties poetry was the predominant literary form in Canada: the few existing publishers were reluctant to take chances with new novelists, as novels were expensive to produce and were thought to have a severely limited audience inside Canada and none whatsoever outside it. But poems could be published as broadsheets, or in one of the five or six "little" magazines then extant, or by very small, frequently self-operated presses; or they could be broadcast on the radio — notably on the CBC's pivotal programme, *Anthology*. Or they could be read aloud.

I first met Gwendolyn MacEwen in the fall of 1960, at The Bohemian Embassy, a coffee house — it was, by then, the age of coffee houses — that featured jazz and folksinging, and, on Thursday nights, poetry readings. The Embassy had the décor of its period — the checked tablecloths, the candles in the chianti bottles; it was also a smoke-filled firetrap. But it was mecca to the poetry community, and MacEwen, who must have been nineteen then, was already a regular reader there. She was a slight-figured, doe-eyed person with long dark hair, who read in an accomplished, sultry, caressing voice that owed, perhaps, a little to Lauren Bacall. The combination of the child-like appearance, the rich voice, and the poetic authority were compelling — you came away from a MacEwen reading feeling you'd been let in on a unique and delicious secret.

MacEwen's primary interest as a poet was in language, and in its corollary, myth-making. In this she was not alone: the late fifties and the early sixties comprised a sort of minor Age of Myth, though there were, of course, other influences around. Northrop Frye's *Anatomy of Criticism* held critical centre stage, with Marshall McLuhan and his structural analysis of popular culture moving up strongly. Leonard Cohen's first volume was called *Let Us Compare Mythologies*; James Reaney's magazine *Alphabet* was entirely devoted to the "mythopoeic" approach, or to correspondences between "real life" and "story"; and Canadian poets were endlessly telling each other that what they really needed to do was to create an "indigenous mythology." In this context, MacEwen's interest in what we might call a mythic structuring of reality — or the structuring of a mythic reality, in opposition to the disappointing world of mundane experience she often refers to as "Kanada" — seems less bizarre. True, no one else settled on Ancient Egypt and the Middle East with quite the same intensity as she does, but her imaginative otherworld is not limited to one time or place. In general — and especially in her earlier poetry — she opposes the works of children, magicians, adventurers, escape artists, the hierarchical and splendid past, the divinely mad, the "barbaric," and poetry, to that of grown-ups, materialists, bureaucrats, the modern daily grind, stolid sanity, the "tame," and newspaper prose.

One of the paradoxes of MacEwen's work is that the protagonists she chooses — in Yeatsean terms, the *personae* — are almost invariably male. She speaks in a female voice when addressing, as the lyric "I", a male "You," but when she uses a more dramatic form, or writes a poem about a heroic figure, the central character is usually a man, such as the escape artist Manzini, or Sir John Franklin, or — in a

later, major work — Lawrence of Arabia. When female fig-
ures from history or story do appear as speakers, they are
likely to be exceptions to their sex: Egyptian princesses, not
ordinary Egyptian women; Rider Haggard's *She*, with her
supernatural powers.

But this is not really surprising. The roles available
to women at the time lacked energy; and if what interest-
ed you was magic, risk, and exploration, rather than, say,
quiet contemplation in the garden between meals, the
choice of a male voice was almost inevitable. MacEwen
wanted to be out on the sharp edge with the boys, not
back in the kitchen with the girls; she was entranced with
cosmic predicaments, and the time for female astronauts
had not yet come. She might have analyzed the female
condition and then tapped the resulting anger, like Sylvia
Plath; but then she would have been a very different kind
of poet. Power — including the dark side of power — was
much more interesting to her than powerlessness. Even in
the love poems, in which she repeatedly invokes and
extols what appears to be a transcendent male figure — a
kind of male muse — it's evident who is doing the invok-
ing; and invoking is after all a kind of conjuring, with suc-
cess dependent on the expertise and verbal skill of the
conjuror. What engaged her was not complaint but exu-
berance, not descent but ascent: not the fire, but the *rising*
fire.

The first volume of Gwendolyn MacEwen's selected
poems covers the first fifteen years of her poetic career,
from the late fifties to the early seventies. It traces the
bright trajectory of her early verse, followed by the aston-
ishingly rapid development and exfoliation of her talent.
In these poems her range and craft, her poetic strength and
intelligence, speak for themselves. Over these years she
created, in a remarkably short time, a complete and diverse

poetic universe and a powerful and unique voice, by turns playful, extravagant, melancholy, daring and profound. To read her remains what it has always been: an exacting but delightful pleasure, though not one without its challenges and shadows.

Deal, infidel, the night is indeed difficult.

M.A., 1993

Gwendolyn MacEwen

Volume One

The Early Years

From ADAM'S ALPHABET, SELAH and *THE DRUNKEN CLOCK*

These first poems are taken from Gwendolyn MacEwen's earliest work, composed when she was under twenty. At an age when most poets are still stumbling through their first stilted and derivative lyrics, they display a preoccupation with form and a sureness of style which is more than precocious.

Adam's Alphabet exists only in manuscript. Hebrew was the first foreign language which caught MacEwen's attention. She was fascinated by the way each letter of its alphabet could also stand for a thing and a nest of associations, which allowed poets writing in it to create complex puns and systems of allusion. *Adam's Alphabet* is MacEwen's set of variations on themes suggested by Psalm 119. Reprinted here is a part of her *Introduction,* and six of the twenty-two poems.

Selah (1961) and *The Drunken Clock* (1961) were both small self-published pamphlets. Most poets of MacEwen's generation began publishing this way, as well as in little magazines. Such small booklets could be sold at readings, and were also carried by some of the more literary bookstores. They were even accorded review space in such journals as *The University of Toronto Quarterly* — so small was the total number of Canadian books published each year.

These poems already display a fluidity, originality and confidence rare at any age, but truly astonishing in a poet under twenty.

ADAM'S ALPHABET

ONE / THE CABALA

Hebrew Acrostics took hold during the Gaonic age; they are at least as old as the 7th century B.C., the time of the Babylonian Exile. In Hebrew literature Acrostics are as abundant . Poets like Judah ha-Levi and the medieval Kalir used them widely for spelling out the name of the poet in letters and writings and so forth. Common too are the Acrostics used for charms and Memnonics as in the Mishnah, the Talmud, etc.

It is, however, in the books of the Cabala, the mystical writing of the Jews, that we find a sense of alphabet, a sense of letter which is a more significant one. The 22 letters of the Hebrew alphabet are given definite interpretation and function — the intriguing concept, for example, that the world was created by these 22 letters. The eternal Tetragrammaton, the creative Word, the ineffable name of God — YHVH — are the four sacred letters which can correspond to the four elements of creation:

Y — yod — life, fire
H — heh — mind, water
V — vau — truth, air
H — heh — love, earth

These in turn were given high pictorial symbolism also in the vision of Ezekiel, where the letters were represented by four animals — lion, eagle, man, ox.

Of the variety and extent of the occult writings using these letters in Hebrew (and Christian Gnostic) literature, I can say little, for the list is endless. The Book of Tokens, written probably by a later Cabalist, is one good example of poetic elaboration and interpretation of the Hebrew letters. Aside from this, the quality of the letters is so deeply rooted in the lore of the Cabala and many other Hebrew sources as to have become an almost literal art. It is perhaps only in the Hebrew language that the value of letters is so extensively, so intrinsically, a part of both religion and culture.

TWO / PSALM 119

The Book of Psalms falls into three rough groups — hymns of praise, elegies, and didactic psalms — and was probably used as a hymn book during the period of the second temple. The post-exilic period was one of intense political and religious turmoil. Psalm 119 bears witness to the frustrations that Hellenism created for pious Jewry.

In the Book of Psalms the Acrostic arrangement was often employed to supply artificial links between verses not logically connected. Psalm 119 is often referred to as the most artificial of the lot. The author, presumably a Pharisaic scribe of the later Greek period in Palestine, employed the Acrostic format — the 22 strophes of the Psalm correspond to the 22 Hebrew letters and each strophe contains eight verses beginning with the same letter which introduces the strophe. A neat, but rather rigid arrangement, which along with the repeated eight synonyms for *Word of God*, one of which occurs in every verse save seven, created a rather monotonous litany, still evident in English.

There is no progress of thought, and such progress would scarcely have been possible under the iron rule which the author imposed upon himself.
(Peake's Commentary on the Bible —1919)

It is still a great tour de force however — God is referred to or addressed in each of the 10 stanzas.

THREE / ADAM'S ALPHABET

The following work is neither a re-write nor a translation. It is a *re-conception* of Psalm 119 which found its genesis in an odd discovery. I was struck with the relationships between the Hebrew letters and their respective strophes. Apart from the obvious Acrostic tie there seemed to be evidence of a more symbolic almost Cabbalistic motive. As one example the letter *samech* (s) means a *prop* and in the *samech* strophe of the psalm I found two indirect references to a prop, its function:

> — *uphold me according to Thy word* 116
> — *hold thou me up and shall be safe* 117

Similarly in *yod* (y) — *yod* means *hand* :

> — *Thy hands have made me and fashioned me* 73

The possibility that these fine symbolic threads were deliberately connected is a slight one. The author was a Pharisee not a Cabbalist. It is probable that they crop up out of coincidence in the English. However, this idea forms the backbone of the following work, a marriage of Pharisee and Cabbalist.

I've tried to maintain, of course, the predominant tones of the Psalm complaint, gloom, and enclose the constituent sections in their *letter-images*, some of which seemed intrinsic; others of which had to be superimposed over the strophes. There is a sort of logical progression, contrary to the quotation in Part Two of the introduction, but it is a purely figurative one: hand-palm-goad; water-fish; etc., and is spasmodic at that, resting for the most part on the natural alphabetical sequence. That sequence is undisturbed; if anything, the parts have been more closely welded.

The psalm has also been transposed into free verse. No exaggerated structural laws cage the natural movement of the content as did the rigid structure cage the original Psalmist.

Modern poets still write psalms. We can celebrate or swim in negations; we can cry out against Greece or Rome, our own oppressive societies, or ourselves. Israel in the clutch of foreign cultures can be Will in the clutch of anything which is foreign to it or which shackles its forward flow; it is all the same cry.

The upper case *He*, perpetual pronoun of the Deity, cannot carry the same implications today as it did in the Psalmist's lifetime. Emotional and intellectual realism rule; call it an appeal to Reason.

GMc

DALETH / THE DOOR

sand-paralleled I reach the house
where is dense white room
and my self hangs humid from the walls.
(straighten this bent daleth:)

pillars to prop the soul's lame body
prop this roof, and I've a heart
such braided knot, no light
would finger through —

get the pulse, grease
the hinged pulse
behind the door . . .

for I wish width, the door of self
mouthed open. Let broaden,
let the heart groan its scarlet
hinge-s
and split the red air wide

BETH / THE HOUSE

the house has haunches
in a ledge of rock; the house harbors
the Unknown like a charged chair
in a room of tensions; I sit;
I hide my lit mind here.

　in order to spring
　we must first genu-
　flect.
(athletes in a tense moment)

let the heart knee the rock; let
the static house　　jump
its boundaries; reason　　leap
the grim pebbles of this day;　the house
holds the word that guards a license
of flight that　　lifts
to old high rainbowed song (a sojourn
in this squat and solemn place,

then pass on)

TETH / THE SNAKE

a greased string, it
sang through the old wheatless years;
pagans used it as a whip for me,
coiled the wired morning. but
their striking
was an inverted virtue
my will strode on; the whip's
affliction stiffened me
for things of a slippery eden,
and another snake — Eve's,
to bare the mind to a testament
involving cancelled light —
the first wrong apple
rotting in a snake's stretched gut.

nor the silver serpent
 count among riches —
  only the fat light,
   the goldgrain syllables
    Your mouth imparts . . .

GAIN / THE WEAPON

in my hand a spear sleeps.
remember Your gift —
the career of this blade . . .

a leaf, I am folded double
between scarlet cains,
their vermin-million, and
though the spear wards off
their
 danced
  advances,
I quiver at their plunged brains,
their vermilion dance, and

thrust —
return with a slice-
d hallelujah singing
the throat of the spear
for You, loud loot of song
and the wide carpet of song
is spread sanely
on the floor of Your sky, Eli.

NUN / THE FISH

fish in the net, the light
hooked up, the snare of days . . .
in the vile net I smile
for small intentions:
net of the loved-law threadwhites!
nor emptied down by fools, nor hold me longer than a
fish's blink in the sea.
I swimsail, praise, nor has the Light in me
been up-hooked by He
who cast another net
for various peccant devilfish.
Eli — accept the fish that shimmers,
stammers of an ocean glory:
swum like waterdancer
in this jellied element —
the laughing amphibian, I
praise You with prayer
like bubble
to the lit
surface!

YOD / THE HAND

fingers in the womb,
in the womb's womb, thumbs
press the hollow palm:
  Your hands scooped me
  from the sung seed, flung flesh
  about the bone house;
  the pelvic cave of stone
  — my structured self,

  the molded embryo blinking
  still was bludgeoned
  with cain's hand
  before birth . . .

wombwounded, but Your fingers
comfort in the excellent rain
of the kind fingers, thumbs
smooth the stubble of brain,
lovehalo a torn head
in this skeleton season.

EVIDENCE OF MONDAY

The flower in the narrow vase
is questionable.
Though no mystery should inflict
the brief boy
entering with apples
into the room of the quick clean line,
come in from the brief earth
he wanders on; he's stumped

by those who paint lilies
in a bright innocent science —
the lily-gilders, coaters
of the question of the flower.

The brief boy entering with apples
on a clean-lined monday
only knows the flower nude; knows it
without vase, knows it narrow,
locked in the brief green world,

knows the hurricane want
that outwipes
the painted skin of each flower
and bundles them to form
a great tied evidence of his
questionable monday
for himself
for him to carry back to the most old garden,
. . . eden under the tugging years,
. . . eden at the end of days

SELAH

First of all,
who pasted the tiger
round about the lily?

And the immense naïveté of hills —
fathered these?
You of the loud talents?

And acres of song
or why song harvests itself
— no various crop —

Elohim, I think you are
a tidbit to tease fine eternity.
(Ssssh, he is the guardian
of the substance of light,
ssssh)

But we (made gentle,
made wild, wondering
tiger lilies and such
and such)

dance on dark obsidian,
heavy twisted lava of our thoughts
made rare and
hot diminutive,

and do not even (hills, song,
poor tiger looped around the lily)
hint You.

So we make rings of laughter,
great apples, make rings of
wild toothed apples,
and after the last colon
of our days, You write
a short and strange "Selah",
summing up all the tigers, and
with the lilies, we

EXPLODES, FOR INSTANCE

the old rose still moves
the day, wired up
in red electric, static pins
its risen stem and
though the old
slush of tradition drags dirt
over the covers
of all the books in crooks
of crooked houses,

our blood fires them
through, explodes, for instance,
the critical mesh
of gone days,

for we are loud
and our lung-loud songs
call up dead gardens (inverted seed)

though a bladdered boy
pees, for instance
on the roses.

CERTAIN FLOWERS

some unthinking god
threw me cold violets last morning
when the rain was a prince in the garden.

said: here, define a certain fear in flowers,
chalk out quickly the peril of beauty,

said softly this, as I worried private light
among the blooms
and stretched a half-winged bird of verse
to band the prince, the bloodless blossoms.

some unthinking god
is made of towering flowers; his eye
in the tall blue tulip sky,
a profound petal there; I arrest its blooming.

!I want the flowers beheaded,
the garden sink,
the rain deny its claim to princedom there

and stand in a garden of void
applauding, tracing the biographies
of brief past flowers, capturing the moment of bloom
in a cage of my own sunlight

EDEN, EDEN

it is the thunder is
the vocal monument
to the death-wished rain;
or obelisk in a granite sky
that roars a jawed epitaph
through cut cloud.

in the morning
thunder is the reared stone elephant,
      the grown element of gray;
its trunk is vertical and thick as thunder;
the elephant stubs down the wrenched lightning,
funnelling a coughed verse
for the suicidal rain
in the morning.

      •   •

the stormed man is heavy with rain
and mumbles beneath the elephant gargle
and his jaw locks human in the rain,
and under the unlocked jaw of the cut sky
and under the bullets of the elephant's trunk

he is thinking of a thunder garden.

Behind sense he is thinking of a warped tree
with heavy fruit falling;
peaked rock fighting the ragged fern
in the other storm's centre;
a monolithic thunder tree
and a man and woman naked and green with rain
above its carved roots, genesis

ROME AND THE JESTERS

the moment's in goliath-miniature
when the rain clears the leaf
and the pinhead titan noon rears
back on its old country,
counting us fools who've just escaped

from trying to essay the morning.
but the boy jests;
let the little boy jest
in his mudworm sandcourt
for King Day
loves his jesters/with a love
surpassing reason

and there's more reason
in the mudboy's sandjest
than's found in our hours of heavy
cal-cu-lus,
fellow pushers, layers of the brick minute,
hammerers on the skin of the old stone hour.

> his sister found 2 apples
> tumbled absurd on the tumbled sandbank
> ;she polished them;
> let the logic of her polished
> whimsy grow
>
> the sophisticated twins (like
> Remus and Romulus

sucking the thin twin teats
of the where-wolf, time-wolf
where today is)
do gain an edge on the morning
for they cover it with slow sand
like a child spooned under the summerbeach,

for they scale the hours
by the growing sheen of apples,
by the accumulative mudcastle.

we have laid all morning
in hopeless minute-bricks.
I must tell you the time, (it's
my foreman's duty, and the jesters
will not understand, of course —
God duly bless those 2 founders
of the rome-ing hour
and God help the suckered she-wolf)

it's noon

THE DRUNKEN CLOCK

The bells ring more than sunday; eve,
orchards and high wishes meet the bells
with grace and speed. The staggered
clocks only cousin the bells; after
the timed food, the urgent breakfasts,
we lean to other seasons. Season

of the first temple
of a basic babel
of sumer
of meek amoeba

Clocks count forward with craze, but
bells count backwards in sober grace.
Tell us, in the high minute after they
sing, where the temple is; where
the bell's beat breaks all our hour-
glass; where the jungled flesh
is tied, bloodroots.

From **THE RISING FIRE**

Gwendolyn MacEwen published both *The Rising Fire*, her first major verse collection, and *Julian the Magician*, her strangely surreal first novel, in 1963, when she was twenty-two. In the same year her work also appeared in John Robert Colombo's landmark anthology, *Poésie/Poetry 64*.

The Rising Fire was published by Contact Press, a small literary house run at that time by poets Raymond Souster, Louis Dudek and Peter Miller. Contact published only poetry, and merely to appear on its list conferred a prestige well beyond the number of books sold. With the appearance of *The Rising Fire*, with its flourishing virtuoso style, its interest in both mysticism and physics, and its landscapes of magical transformation, MacEwen was firmly established on the literary map. But then, as ever, she was a member of no school or movement other than her own.

Asked for a comment at the time, she wrote, "My life and work are so interrelated that one always implies and defines the other. Poetry is the first love, but prose is the strong undercurrent. I still feel extremely embryonic. As the horizons of the world widen for me the poetry moves parallel, shifting, forming new complexities and sudden simplicities."

> *look how we live —*
> *with what outrageous energy —*

THE BREAKFAST

under the knuckles of the warlord sun how long do we have
how long do we have, you ask, in the vast magenta wastes
of the morning world when the bone buckles under for war
when the bone intersects as tangents in the district of the sun
centipedes and infidels; snakes and the absence of doves?

a breakfast hysteria; perhaps you have felt it,
the weight of the food you eat, the end of the meal coming
before you lift the spoon; or eat only apples
to improvise an eden. or forget the end takes place
in each step of your function.

look, the spoon is lifted halfway through invisible tables
of dangerous logarithms in the abstract morning spaces;
come, come — eat leviathans in the breakfast wastelands
eat bestiaries and marine zoos and apples and avaries.
by eating the world you may enclose it.

seek simplicities; the fingerprints of the sun only
and the fingernail of the moon duplicating you in your body,
the cosmos fits your measures; has no ending;

place one hand before the sun and make it smaller,
hold the spoon in your hand up to the sky
and marvel at its relative size; comfort yourself
with the measures of a momentary breakfast table.

ah lord sun
ah terrible atomic breakfast
ah twilight of purple fallout
ah last deck of evening cards —
deal, infidel, the night is indeed difficult

THE MOUNTAIN: A STUDY IN RELATIVE REALITIES

the staccato from the gut
like sunset guns, the way we stutter
cryptic causalities and command queer reasons
for mountains based on smashed senses — eyes
like screens, ears like blocked harbors, skulls
like tonal caves which echo altogether too much
and hearts like red whales behind the fishbone ribs
which are boorish and stupid and fly our brains
like kites

is too much. Ah
in our weird apocalyptic sceneries, whimsies
and filigreed senses define little after all;
a mountain is an inviolate triangle in an offhand
way, vaguely difficult to handle in a manual
sense, but our sunset faces are sweet landscapes
with rosy retinae and receptive nostrils and
it is too soon to think of halfway vision and
the questions of perception of an inverted people
etcetera.

The mountain . . . say
imagine we could double it or make an octave
of mountain or generally manipulate things concave
or convex or whatever, an amusing distraction
like war or dominoes, though somewhere the point
is lost. But now you watch me through your sunset
senses for you expected a poem and prose is suggested.
O men mouthing staccato causalities, O women with
queer cryptic reasons for all things — I grant
it is difficult in these equivocal Canadian sunsets
to imagine that through your senses you do indeed
invent the mountain.
Anyhow, absurd,
but it does serve literature.
Anyone for tea before the night falls?

UNIVERSE AND: THE ELECTRIC GARDEN

the protons and the neutrons move, gardener,
sire their sons, spirals of sense,
and servant their planets,
their negative pebbles
in a pool of moons; electrons like
mad bees
        circle;
              the nuclei reach out
to harness them;
              will of the sun reach out,
strap earth, strap moon, slowly excite
other stars, set, set the sweet fanatic pace
going;
        telescopes turn inward, bend down.

In our gardens are electric roses
which spark, push light, push fuchsia
in flailing grass

and spines of long magnetic seas cloy . . .
rake their depths for dust; all holds;
the spines hold the elemental jelly
of the sea's; flesh there . . .

I walk warily through
my electric garden

POEM

I acknowledge you, I —
skied down slopes of snow
our bare bones fabled and born
from the torchlit rooms of cities,
our brows powdered and raised
in perpetual amazement, I
acknowledge you, I
and the tunnels of our mouths
being strange passages.

bleakly the snow confesses
its sterile histories, I
acknowledge you, I
and the feet skiing down it
under the cobalt riddles
of winter skies and
the fingers of our hands being
islands perpetually discovered.

I acknowledge you, I
and the penciling green worm
under islands of cities
and sterile snows, making
sensual tunnels and
atrocious labyrinths and
terrible reason.

I acknowledge you, I —
fearfully in poetry or otherwise
and my voice involves trumpets —

an elephant's trunk
or a trunk of a thunder tree —
look how we live —
with what outrageous energy —

THE DEATH AGONY OF THE BUTTERFLY

a monarch beat its velvet brain
against the light, against
the cold light, I
thought of you.

dance you, dance
you bitch
against the light against
the cold light, that's
what you said.

always behind me, always
behind me is
your violent music, beat
until the butterfly's velvet brain
is dead

dance you, dance
you bitch, I
love you against
the light against
the cold light, always
behind me is
your violent music.

SKULLS AND DRUMS

you talked about sound, not
footstep sound, shiphorn, nightcry,
                                        but

strings collecting, silver
and catgut, violas riding
the waves of May like soft ships,
                                        yes

and the anchoring senses,
the range, the register,
the index
            in the ear; the long
measure from the drums of our skulls
to the heart (and its particular tempo);
the music anchored there, gathered
in.

you will hear me now, I think,
while my skin still gathers tones of the sun in,
while we ride the bars, the slow passages
of these first minutes;

while the taut drums of our skulls
open
and all sounds enter
and the pores of our skin like slow valves open.

we will hear each other now, I think,
while nothing is known, while sound
and statement in the ear

leave all alternatives;

> our skulls like drums,
> like tonal caves
> echo, enclose.

while the ribs of our bodies are great hulls
and the separate ships of our senses
for a minute

anchor.

for a minute in the same harbor

anchor.

INQUIRY INTO TIME

The little boy has left the crowd,
left your tight handclasp
at noon in nineteen-sixty.
Where has the little boy gone?

You have given him mint and wishes.
It does not matter.
You have given him large toys and large love.
It does not matter. He does not want them.

The little boy has gone to the coliseum
to watch the gold chariots.
He has gone to gaze on red Roman nostrils
of rare Roman horses.

Why did the little boy go? from your hand?
out of the crowd?
You have given him custard and bicycles.
And it does not matter. He does not want them.

He heaved his ball into the coliseum
and has gone to sit with Caesar's son
and watch the gold chariots; I told you.

You have given him scooters and embroidered pillows.
It does not matter.
He has centuried away from you
to play ball in gold-toned Rome
and sit with Caesar's son above the chariots.

The hand on your clock melts like a Dali,
the years chew their nails, worried that one boy
has seen through their pretense.
Then you must melt also, here in the one noon;
melt like that clock, like that boy's clock
to follow him

THE MAGICIAN: THREE THEMES

One: The Magician

odd that the people want to own you
and produce you like a black poodle
at fatal teaparties where their blood crowds
up in the thunder of the afternoon,
inside their houses, in the fatal rooms
of their faith and dark doubting.
pull the shades of their windows
and give them what they want which is
the brilliance of their own darkness,
their shrouded blood hooked out
on gleaming master fisherman's wires
for the dance of the ultimate arteries
and the brain's calypso and the shifting
of their minds' hard shadows.

Two: The Magician as Man

but it's irksome spending whole afternoons
producing pearly rabbits
for the lettuce-patches of any house
when my real love is the mind
moving as sailboat through the days,
the whiteness and the freedom of it.

Three: The Magician as Christ

yet like penicillin from a mould
his pretense breeds wonder
at the throat of their belief
like fingers or a strange bacteria
holds the hard mind screaming;
the crust and the context of his act
holds in bright hypnosis
the white of their brains
and the dark of their veins, how
much of him is theirs, how much of him
do they re-create in the vast thunderous churches
of their need . . .

THE TOWN CRIER

we would have gone to the campaign but
we had been born in turfs and stables
with foxes speaking beneath the stars and
syrup anointing Canadian maples; O
it was the sound of the city that took us
out from under the champagne heavens
to the brink of asphalt and concrete
raggedly as backward gypsies as
epileptic people in the season of our need.

      — how first the stones spoke
of permanence, as petrified trees
built in blocks; the steady geometry
of it, and the laughter from gutters
and rooftops always; we were old
and suddenly infinite in the city;
Christ fell from our lips
and our heels like a dog like
an undigested meal; the bay of Toronto
made waterrings at our ankles —

O Samsons and 12 o'clock saints
O shopkeepers crooked in our elbows
like lambs — did we think
to deliver you? Slowly and slowly
the city rose beyond us;
it was a myth that grew like a weed
in the season of our need,
until one day a man wearing

cloaks of yellow and wild maroon
rang a gong in the trafficked noon
and cried news of tomorrow;
though the cars ate his voice away
and he could not be heard, we were absurd
on that terrible day; I remember
running out to the brink
of the asphalt and concrete
with tar on our feet and dirt
on our temples, out like old men
to the turf and the stables.

THE DIMENSIONS OF A TIGER

the cat in the grass lengthens —
and your tendons reach widely
into seasons of wind and deltas —
you are suddenly aware that
you have no boundaries, that
you are a field with no fences.

hollyhock and frolic, you
are the width of wind and voices
until something, a microscopic irony
as laughter breaking from windows
or a diminutive rain shrinks you
and the cat in the grass curls under

THE CIRCUS

and somehow they
dance in their aquamarine
sequins, the acrobats.
seeming that in their
slow grotesque arabesque
there is great pain
in the turning,
the hands clutching
and the loins touching
for macabre contact finally
and the music is all
absurd for them.

turning, I
see myself floundering
double in your eyes, in
the brights of them;
two of me repeated
in aquamarine mirrors and
know the grotesque
plural you
is mirrored in mine also.

in all, pain. in all
the slow acrobatic dance
behind our eyes
in the skull's circus.
forgive me then
that even this
— your pain —
is a poem.

THE FERRIS WHEEL

long among the holiness of saints
with salmon eyes and slender fingers
I ask you to revise your codes of holiness,
in horn and halo, I
ask you to join me on
the ferris wheel.

and to be circular and have no level
nor total logic nor anchoring of orders
but be in movement, nor static circle,
worlds from the still middle, the
point of absolute inquiry
and stop nowhere on the mind's circumference.

to be holy as with scabs on the knees
and snot in the nose always, not
one minute of your move will define you
at any time, I
ask you to join me on
the ferris wheel.

THE PHOENIX

For D.

beyond you, the image rising from the shoulders
is greater than you, as the phoenix from the fire
is risen, as the rising fire on the opening wings
is greater than the stirring and potential pyre.

you appear in the weekdays of your wishes
or musical Sundays and make on an instrument's strings
idly, high harmonics which transcend the note
and will not believe that these are also wings.

enter and re-enter the burning of your city
in the heat of the weekday, with anything enter
innocently lyric, with gravity, or phallic,
with you who are beautiful and difficult to suffer.

observe that your anatomy is fire and brains are ashes
and in the terms of old madness, sleep with queens;
take root; the most available loins are here
to place the equivocal seeds between.

circuses of knees, and the bone trapezes
out from its first wish to the bone of another —
past the most pleasant of all anatomies
where one trapeze succeeds the other —

MORNING LAUGHTER

To my mother, Elsie MacEwen

umbilical I lumbered
trailing long seed, unwombed
to the giant vagina, unarmed,
no sprung Athene
— cry, cry in the sudden salt
of the big room, world
— I uncurled plastic limbs of senses,
freed the crashing course of menses,
                    — hurled

I hurled the young tongue's spit
for a common coming, a genesis
sans trumpets and myrrh, rejected
whatever seed in love's inside
fought and formed me from
an exodus of semen come
  for the dream of Gwen,
  the small one,
  whose first salt scream
heralded more and borrowed excellence.

years have tied the sweet cord;
morning laughter, ships of daughter
and of mother move together
in clumsy grace:
you look to a roof of brass clouds
crash loud as the known world knows us;
and each motion's intrinsic as I reach
beyond roofs for a clutch of that first seed.

wary we speak from a fringe of meanings,
circle and pat-a-cake in cat-paw diplomacy,
each hope hoisted to a veined rainbow,
our common denominator, whose colors
are all blood and bone,

wary we speak from a fringe of meanings,
each tongue censored with love and its
cat-paw circling
      ,now foetal in the world's wide womb
      ,now known in my own rebellious belly
       the stuff to people further days
      ,now forced by some grim reason
       to hark down the bonds of the blood
      ,can still remember from that womb walking,
       sideways out of that womb,
       glorious from that womb, bent and insolent.

— morning laughter with your young daughter —
smile at the pen she picks, armed to bring light
into terrible focus
and the paper builds worlds but makes
no prodigal . . .

who would erase the scribbled slate
of gone years, their jumbled algebra,
their rude designs
junked under a rainbow, all blood and bone
that links the mother and the morning daughter —
and acknowledge now, armed and still insolent
that what is housed in the fragile skull
— light or learning or verbal innocence —
grows from the woman somehow who housed the whole
body,
who first fed the vessels, the flesh and the sense.

FOR ALICK MACEWEN: d. 1960

what we have left behind us in the fathering clay
the finishing bed where the veins flow grey
in the grave unequivocal, is little, redundancy.

long long beneath the morning moon of our halfway
vision, our wrong repent repeats, stalls
the noon coming, is wrong recalling.

(stolen stolen by the thieves of gravity,
the inverse womb, the inward worm, etc.
O God forgive us these, etc.)

but say you chase life the way you chase
the sunset in grey jets on sunday still
though an organist's veins are opening

for the last warm music; you
were classic somewhere in Canada on sunday
touching trees where old apples fall and birds occur —

(give us that particular cruelty necessary
to take it, your life, a second time, it is
time to speak the truth, it is time to speak,
it is time)

THE CATALOGUES OF MEMORY

1.

now in our distorted distances
the ignorant ships
kiss
and pass

love we have learned nothing
we have learned
nothing
not in the slated nights
not in the chalkboard cities

Jesus, Nietsche, call them
and they will not come for you
though your hair is on fire
from the brain beneath it burning

love we have learned nothing
we have learned
nothing
not on the gold island
not on the washed beaches

we were two ships of burning glass
we were two ships of burning glass

now in our distorted distances
the ignorant ships
kiss
and pass

2.

endangered
you
the strokes of the sun were
lashes to your lips your
brow
beauty burning in
the fires of your room

ah what do I speak
I with pencils
what do I speak
who love you
under fire and churches
in snow
in rainlight
even behind the seasons

sunday somewhere you were
red and gold on beaches
disturbed with gulls
and steamers

monday somewhere you were
gay among ruins
old stone the fake
architecture of Kingsmere
dancing the colors were
Fall the colors fell
into your hair into
your brow etc.

ah who am I with pencils
who love you
behind reason
behind the poem
even behind the seasons
defining as the poem pillages
reason, you who defy the reasons
of poetry, you endangered
by your own images

3.

your hand on my left breast
perhaps, or the ankles
staying; the genitals like tears;
your eyes wide with fear.
the attack.
lions . . . the lean loins of them,
we were ships, we were lions, we
were delicate with our images,
we were man in a blind man's vision
and our name was adam and we had no home.

always always was your face moving
before the ships before the buildings,
a crescent leaning, the conscience
of the flesh.

now it is winter; heed, heed
I say, heed
the speech of your hands.
feet, feet, I say,
move swiftly,
leave
no track

THE CHOICE

and so we have a choice of several deaths.

death one, the catapult farflung wish
               from the stomach or the skullcave
               shot like a bat out of belfries
               or various hells, like a horse
               through a landscape of cardboard
               calendars.

death two, it is lovely, it is lovely
               the second death, you
               do not even know it, you
               just fold up on a subway
               like yesterday's newspaper
               until someone picks you up
               not bothering to read you.

death three, it is dirty, it is dirty
               the third death because
               you plan it. it offends
               people, it is offensive, a car
               from a cliff, a hole behind
               the eyes, a drug dream.

and so we have a choice of several deaths
and that in itself is a consolation.
so go to it love, go to it:
the red of the flower your fingers are holding,
the green in the speech of your mouth;
drive it, drive the horse through landscapes
like calendars of cardboard, or nonsense mosaics
for we are great statements in our days

and on the basis of that we can expect small audiences.

GENERATION COMETH

the boy
a coy root or
bright among cities
is growing you
cannot stop him you
cannot stop him
growing.

try to
pull him out
by the roots
from your loins he
is green like a tree
planted there

he is in your dark garden
he will eat your dark flowers
you cannot stop him old
men old women you
cannot stop him
growing.

his thumb his
bright brain his
heel is beneath you
send him to school
or macabre churches you
cannot stop him

not even the wild
Muria boy stood
wild and white-toothed
among jungles
and found them
complicated —

he grows beneath your heels
and the city for him is easy he
knows it from below
old men old women you
cannot stop him
growing.

From A BREAKFAST FOR BARBARIANS

A Breakfast for Barbarians was published by Ryerson Press in 1966. In 1965, Gwendolyn MacEwen won the CBC's New Canadian Writing award for poetry. It was a high-energy period for her, though not all of her experiences were positive: during some of this time she was pursuing a divorce from her first husband, poet Milton Acorn, whom she had married in 1962.

A Breakfast for Barbarians is MacEwen's single most accomplished collection of poems. Of it, she wrote:

"These poems arise out of a wilful hunger, a deep involvement with self and world, a belief that to live consciously is holy, while merely to exist is sacrilege . . .

"Here is a book of poems — or call it a menu. A breakfast menu, breakfast being a more profound and sacramental meal than supper, because after all it's the first meal; it's the pact you make with yourself to see the day through.

"I should like to think these poems have a certain value for what I term their essential "optimism" . . . I write basically to communicate joy, mystery, passion, not the joy that naively exists without knowledge of pain, but that joy which arises out of and conquers pain. I want to construct a myth . . . "

my friends my sweet barbarians,
there is that hunger which is not for food

A BREAKFAST FOR BARBARIANS

my friends, my sweet barbarians,
there is that hunger which is not for food —
but an eye at the navel turns the appetite
round
with visions of some fabulous sandwich,
the brain's golden breakfast
                    eaten with beasts
                    with books on plates

let us make an anthology of recipes,
let us edit for breakfast
our most unspeakable appetites —
let us pool spoons, knives
and all cutlery in a cosmic cuisine,
let us answer hunger
with boiled chimera
and apocalyptic tea,
an arcane salad of spiced bibles,
tossed dictionaries —
                    (O my barbarians
                    we will consume our mysteries)

and can we, can we slake the gaping eye of our desires?
we will sit around our hewn wood table
until our hair is long and our eyes are feeble,
eating, my people, O my insatiates,
eating until we are no more able
to jack up the jaws any longer —

to no more complain of the soul's vulgar cavities,
to gaze at each other over the rust-heap of cutlery,

drinking a coffee that takes an eternity —
till, bursting, bleary,
we laugh, barbarians, and rock the universe —
and exclaim to each other over the table
over the table of bones and scrap metal
over the gigantic junk-heaped table:

by God that was a meal

THE GARDEN OF SQUARE ROOTS :
AN AUTOBIOGRAPHY

and then the rattlesnake spines of men distracted me
for even they, the people were
as Natajara was, who danced
while I was anchored like a passive verb
or Neptune on a subway —

and from the incredible animal i
grew queer claws inward to fierce cribs;
I searched gardens for square roots,
for i was the I interior
the thing with a gold belt and delicate ears
with no knees or elbows
was working from the inside out

this city I live in I built with bones
and mortared with marrow;
I planned it in my spare time
and its hydro is charged from a blood niagara
and I built this city backwards and
the people evolved out of the buildings
and the subway uterus ejected them —

for i was the I interior
the thing with a gold belt and delicate ears
with no knees or elbows
was working from the inside out.

and all my gardens grew backwards
and all the roots were finally square
and Ah! the flowers grew there like algebra

THE HOUSE

in this house poems are broken,
I would invent the end of poetry;
we are only complete when

> that image of me in you
> that image of you in me
> breaks, repairs itself.

you are the earth and the earth;
release those cosmic hands which held you
while I set out on my urgent journeys —

> in this house we repair
> torn walls together and do not
> ask how they were torn.

we work slowly, for
the house is the earth
and the earth —

> the delicate people in you
> move
> from room to room.

IT RAINS, YOU SEE

Reader, I do not want to complicate the world
but mathematics is tragic, there is pathos in numbers;
it's all over, boys — space is curved,
you are hungry and your hunger multiplies by hundreds.

in your first shuddering temple of chalk
in the slate days you taught numbers
to jive under the complex chewing pencils; you talked
darkly of the multiplying world, and your fingers

hunted for braille like urgent forms.
you go outside and now it rains,
and the rain is teaching itself its own name;
it rains, you see, but Hell it comes down cuneiform.

STRANGE BREAKFAST

I have eaten
strange breakfasts
with you.

Insatiate. These breakfasts
have broken the past
of smashed appetites;
that colossal intake
of morning images
has made me insatiate (ah you
and your colored hungers
who doth enclose my life and my death
in your coffee — friend,
we cannot live too long)

obviously we are preparing for some final feast,
obviously our bellies stretch
for a supreme reason, obviously
we can stomach anything now, anything.

that these breakfasts have broken the past
hungers, hungers that were controlled,
controlled hungers, that these breakfasts
have broken them, that everyone does not wish
executed fish and fried eggs,
that the full belly means only
a further hunger, that we cannot now return
to younger appetites, that we can no longer
eat the bright ancestral food,
that we alone must set all our tables single-handed,

that we alone must account for the grease of our spoons
that we alone must wash our mouths
that we alone must look back and decline
all dinner offers,
that we alone will walk into the city at 9 o'clock
knowing that the others have also eaten
knowing that there is no time to compare the contents
of our bodies in our cities
that we eat and we eat and we know and we know
that machines work faster than the machines of our mouths

is why our breakfasts
get stranger and stranger.

YOU CANNOT DO THIS

you cannot do this to them, these are my people;
I am not speaking of poetry, I am not speaking of art.
you cannot do this to them, these are my people.
you cannot hack away the horizon in front of their eyes.

the tomb, articulate, will record your doing,
I will record it also, this is not art,
this is a kind of science, a kind of hobby,
a kind of personal vice like coin collecting.

it has something to do with horses
and signet rings and school trophies,
it has something to do with the pride of the loins,
it has something to do with good food and music,
and something to do with power, and dancing.
you cannot do this to them, these are my people.

THE KINDLED CHILDREN

in summer you invoked a fire for children —
you aimed a small lens at the sun and kindled a twig
beneath it. You had that much time to do it —
that much of a magnified afternoon for the children's kindling.

now this innocence confounds me, this ability to stand
hours beneath the prolonged sun, expanding light
in the exploding novum of their eyes, and
without anger at the world's turn, its argument into night.

impossible to know where your anger lies!
in my burning world I must protract time
down to the worlds of my fevered hands
holding knives to carve the lithic minutes of my lines.

and in the kindling unquiet of my brain I recall
all kinds of burning times — a night in fall
when suns went silently nova, light years beyond
your unlit room, and other times, but always the burning

ensues upon my watching you, in summer and in other seasons
when you do not argue the day into night, as I do,
when you hook a whole afternoon into a small lens
and change it into fire for the kindled children,
when you move about, having little need
of wider fires, whole burning worlds, or anything
beyond the intact moments of your deeds.

THE CHILDREN ARE LAUGHING

It is monday and the children are laughing
The children are laughing; they believe they are princes
They wear no shoes; they believe they are princes
And their filthy kingdom heaves up behind them

The filthy city heaves up behind them
They are older than I am, their feet are shoeless
They have lived a thousand years; the children are laughing
The children are laughing and their death is upon them

I have cried in the city (the children are laughing)
I have worn many colors (the children are laughing)
They are older than I am, their death is upon them
I will wear no shoes when the princes are dying

POEM IMPROVISED AROUND A FIRST LINE*

the smoke in my bedroom which is always burning
worsens you, motorcycle Icarus;
you are black and leathery and lean and
you cannot distinguish between sex and nicotine

anytime, it's all one thing for you —
cigarette, phallus, sacrificial fire —
all part of that grimy flight
on wings axlegreased from Toronto to Buffalo
for the secret beer over the border —

now I long to see you fullblown and black
over Niagara, your bike burning and in full flame
and twisting and pivoting over Niagara
and falling finally into Niagara,
and tourists coming to see your black leather wings
hiss and swirl in the steaming current —

now I long to give up cigarettes
and change the sheets on my carboniferous bed;
O baby, what Hell to be Greek in this country
without wings, but burning anyway

The first line around which it was improvised has disappeared.

THE SELF ASSUMES

not love, lean and frequent,
but the accurate earth,
a naked landscape, green
yet free of seasons
is a name the violate self assumes
after its violent beginnings

not this complex dance of fire and blood
which burns the night to morning,
these hypnotic feet which turn us
know no end and no returning

but a fish within a brilliant river
whose body separates the dreaming waters
and never touches land
is a name the violate self assumes
as silver winds instruct the swimmer
who swims with neither feet nor hands

O not this double dance which burns the night to morning
and cracks the latitudes of time and sleep
whose lean and frequent fires in their burning
break apart the landscapes of a dream,
but the accurate self which burns, and burning, assumes green.

THE LEFT HAND AND HIROSHIMA

asked once why I fanned my fingers before my eyes
to screen the strange scream of them, I, sinister, replied:
Recently I dropped a bomb upon Hiroshima.

as for the mad dialectics of my tooth-chewed hands
I knew nothing; the left one was responsible and
abominably strong, bombed the flower of Hiroshima.

only because my poems are lies do they earn the right
to be true, like the lie of that left hand at night
in the cockpit of a sad plane trailing God in its wake.

all the left hands of your bodies, your loud thumbs
did accomplice me! men women children at the proud womb,
we have accomplished Hell. Woe Hiroshima . . .

you have the jekyll hand you have the hyde hand
my people, and you are abominable; but now I am in proud and
in uttering love I occur four-fingered and garbed
in a broken gardener's glove over the barbed
                          garden
                          of Hiroshima . . .

POEM

the slow striptease of our concepts
        — it is even this which builds us,
for you I would subtract my images
        for the nude truth beneath them

as you, voluptuous, as with mirrors at the loins
        are unclothed piece by piece until
each cloth is slander to your skin and
        nakedness itself is silk across your rising sex

SUBLIMINAL

in that sublayer of sense
where there is no time
no differentiation of identities
but co-presents, a static recurrence
(that wolf is stone,
this stone is wolf)

your bones have interlocked
behind my brow
your meanings are absolute
you do not move
but are always moving

in that substratum I hold,
unfold you at random;
your eye is a giant
overflowing me;
your foot is planted
in the marrow of my bone,
today is tomorrow.

vision does not flinch
perspective is not jarred
you do not move
but are always moving

you do not move but are always moving
Christ O Christ no one lives long
along that layer;
I rise to see you planted

in an earth outside me,
moving through time
through the terms of it,
moving through time again
along its shattered latitudes

THE BEAD SPECTRUM

you laugh you cry you wear bright beads
and the colors love you, dozens
huddle upon you.

O lady, the world will not confess your colors
and nowhere are your beads acknowledged
against the spectrum of your city.

but your beads love you
and form their own spectrum
and your fingers fumble them
(infra-red to your throat's final violet)
as colors clash
and all the world's unspeakable accessories
shake like a stripper's machines
and its large horny music
exits you to nakedness.

now in your plural world
your colors huddle, confess themselves
upon your flesh (a pallid apocalypse) —
dynamos crash, and in your room sewing,
you laugh you cry you wear bright beads.

DO YOU HAVE THE TIME

maybe we could determine it by advanced calculus
now that our watches are broken
or by resorting to complicated instruments
now that our clocks are broken
or making clepsydras and sundials
to pour time, shave time, save time
in the steel city, in its sunday streets
whose neutral pavements rush up to meet
the falling bodies of gods and clockmakers
in the morning, before church.

especially on sundays I want to hark
back to the mad instant preceding me,
for I too, no doubt, am an accident
of timing, like a million others
(whole continents are populated by
errors of calendars and clocks) —
yet still they give children
watches on their birthdays,
and they consult their own small wrists
to find out where they stand
(do you have the time? O how
can we tell, who live despite it?
Besides, we buried our watches in the sand).

THE PEANUT BUTTER SANDWHICH

we are dangerous at breakfast, at breakfast we
        investigate the reasons for our myths
viciously, and at breakfast we need no reasons
        for being; we are

solemnly eating our thick sandwiches
        and knowing the highest mysticism
is this courageous breakfast and us at it
        concentrating
        conscious

of our outrageous reality. The sandwich!
        The peanut butter sandwich!
a symbol of itself only, and you beautiful
        across the table, eating.

but caught in this cliché of a breakfast
        and knowing it too, we speak
loudly: "Feed me some symbolisms!
        I want a dragon sandwich!"

"I am freight train, sea-wind and raspberry jam!"
"I am snow, tiger and peanut butter!"

alas, we have too many myths
        and we know that too. but it is breakfast.
I am with you. care for another?

THE MAGICIAN

for Raymond Lowe

finally then the hands must play mad parables
finally then, the fingers' genius
wave out what my poems have said;
finally then must the silks occur
                        plus rabbits
and the big umbrellas be
spun on stage continually.

as you Lowe, in quiet irony
inspire terrible skills of silks
                 or crash scarves vertically
as though miniature brains were held in fingertips
fantastic as of secrecy —

or my art being more a lie anyway
than the lie of these illusions
secreting realities in the twitching silks
or sacred sleeves
                to twist or tamper them
to come out solid, in cubes or cups —
pull down then
               silk avalanche of scarves
or play the cosmos on strings of human hair
                  as a wand cracks
and blinds belief and holds it knotted
        like an ugly necklace
        or a hopeless rope —

or you, Lowe, driving a spike through the head of a boy
as though magic were (and is)
a nail of steel to split the skull

                                in either direction

to believe or not believe
is not the question.

finally then do all my poems become as crazy scarves
issuing from the fingers in a colored mesh
and you, magician, stand as they fly around you
silent as Houdini who could escape from anything
except the prison of his own flesh.

MANZINI: ESCAPE ARTIST

now there are no bonds except the flesh; listen —
there was this boy, Manzini, stubborn with
gut stood with black tights and a turquoise
leaf across his sex

and smirking while the big
brute tied his neck arms legs, Manzini
naked waist up and white with sweat

struggled. Silent, delinquent, he
was suddenly all teeth and knee, straining slack
and excellent with sweat, inwardly

wondering if Houdini would take as long
as he; fighting time and the drenched
muscular ropes, as though his tendons were worn
on the outside —

as though his own guts were the ropes
encircling him; it was beautiful. it was thursday; listen —
there was this boy, Manzini

finally free, slid as snake from
his own sweet agonized skin, to throw his entrails
white upon the floor
with a cry of victory —

now there are no bonds except the flesh,
but listen, it was thursday, there was this boy,
Manzini —

THE WINEMAKER

for Alfred Purdy

the winemaker comes to Toronto
the urgent winemaker comes
        from a little rural cottage
comes to Toronto (can't stand the place, just
        passing through)
with fingers dyed a deep magenta from the stubborn grapes
with one foot on the pavement
and the other poised for flight —

the winemaker invades Toronto
and the city ignites under his heels
        and in a few hours he has accomplished
everything and condenses all possible
        appointments into urgent minutes wherein
the entire history of Canadian poetry
is brought up to date over tavern draught
        or that purple homemade stuff
that dyes the guts a deep magenta —

the winemaker comes to Toronto
        disguised as a dervish to chase himself
back and forth across the urgent purple city, a living query
of his own movement — like those poems of his that go
        round and round and where they stop nobody
guesses —

the winemaker comes to Toronto
(can't stand the place just passing through)
        and leaves a pile of urgent

poems in his wake and leaves again
        for the little rural cottage
back to the deep magenta twilight of Ameliasburg
to write those poems that turn and keep turning

            (there is the man. he returns,
            he is always   returning)

THE THING IS VIOLENT

Self, I want you now to be
violent and without history,
for we've rehearsed too long our ceremonial ballet
and I fear my calm against your exquisite rage.

I do not fear that I will go mad
but that I may not, and the shadows of my sanity
blacken out your burning; act once
and you need not act again —
give me no ceremony, scars are not pain.

The thing is violent, nothing precedes it,
it has no meaning before or after —
sweet wounds which burn like stars,
stigmata of the self's own holiness,
appear and plot new zodiacs upon the flesh.

APPENDECTOMY

it's interesting how you can brag about a scar;
I'm fascinated with mine; it's diagonal and straight,
it suggests great skill, great speed,
it is no longer or shorter than it needs to be.

it is good how it follows my natural symmetry
parallel to the hip, a perfect geometry;
it is not a wound; it is a diagram
drawn correctly, it has no connection with pain.

it's interesting how you can brag about a scar;
nothing in nature is a straight line
except this delightful blasphemy on my belly;
the surgeon was an Indian, and beautiful, and holy.

FINALLY LEFT IN THE LANDSCAPE

Finally left in the landscape is the dancer;
    all maps have resigned, the landscape has
designed him. My lines can only
    plagiarize his dance.

    Moving, he is the cipher of movement,
    a terrific code,
    witness him.

Now I seek him, nor rely on chance,
I turn stones and find broken glass
like pseudo-suns in the broken sand
intense for their size
(are they from his fallen eyes?)

Life, your trillions people me,
I am a continent, a violated geography,
Yet still I journey to this naked country
to seek a form which dances in the sand.
This is my chosen landscape.
Hear my dark speech, deity.

THE ARISTOCRACIES

You are born with these in your blood —
natural aristocracies, not power aristocracies
as the world sees them, but natural aristocracies
evident from the curve of the mouth, from the stance.

The title you confer upon yourself, a pre-occupation
with eagles, a passion for gold, for mountains
for that which is super-natural, superlative,
grants you your maps and your kingdoms.

Let it be understood, this is not art,
this is not poetry; the poetry is
the breathing air embracing you,
the poetry is not here, it is elsewhere
in temples, in territories of pure blue.

Behind my eye a diagonal arabic music
insists I censure dimensions; I think
in cross-sections of sound, flat arabesques;
love, I think you have become a bas-relief.

Can you not break from this censured landscape?
I waste each blue breath from my mouth
and I cannot recover the exiled minutes of my life —
(ruthless, and royal blue the profiles of kings
confound me)

The body of God and the body of you
dance through the same diagonal instant
of my vision. Let this be the end of argument,
O crowned and captive dancer, let me not argue
your flesh to death.

You must dance forever beneath this heavy crown
in an aristocratic landscape, a bas-relief of living bone.
And I will altogether cease to speak
as you do a brilliant arabesque within the bas-relief,
your body bent like the first letter
of an unknown, flawless alphabet.

TERROR AND EREBUS: A VERSE PLAY

Terror and Erebus, although written and broadcast in the early sixties, appeared in print form only in 1974, in the magazine *The Tamarack Review*, and in book form in *Afterworlds* (McClelland and Stewart, 1987).

In the sixties, the CBC commissioned several verse plays from Gwendolyn MacEwen. The writing of these plays was a source of income for her, since money was always a problem. Lacking even a high school diploma, she couldn't — like many poets — teach in a university, nor did she wish to. During this period she supported herself mostly through part-time jobs and a few arts grants, and by giving many readings.

Terror and Erebus is a remarkable text — in its extraordinary language, in its metaphoric leaps and connections. The CBC rendition, with its electronic music and whistling-wind sound effects, was a hair-raising experience. For the story MacEwen went to the nineteenth-century Franklin expedition in search of the Northwest Passage, which has haunted the Canadian imagination for years. In her hands it becomes, not a quest for a quick road to Eastern Money, which is what it was, nor a mournful tale of loss, as in folksongs, but a courageous though doomed venture into the metaphysical Otherworld.

MacEwen re-created the historical Franklin as the kind of hero she loved: daring, adventurous, wilful, maintaining his own version of reality even in the "white asylum" of the Arctic, and in the face of death.

> *The eye* creates *the horizon,*
> *The ear* invents *the wind,*
> *The hand reaching out from a parka sleeve*
> *By touch demands that the touched thing be.*

TERROR AND EREBUS

A Verse Play For Radio

❖

The Speakers —

> RASMUSSEN
> FRANKLIN
> GROZIER
> QAQORTINGNEQ

❖

Roaring wind which fades out to Rasmussen

RASMUSSEN:

King William Island . . . latitude unmentionable.
But I'm not the first here.
They preceded me, they marked the way
                with bones
White as the ice is, whiter maybe,
The white of death,
                of purity . . .

But it was almost a century ago
And sometimes I find their bodies

Like shattered compasses, like sciences
Gone mad, pointing in a hundred directions
                    at once —
The last whirling graph of their agony.
How could they know what I now know,
A century later, my pockets stuffed with
                    comfortable maps —
That this was, after all, an island,
That the ice can camouflage the straits
And drive men into false channels,
Drive men
                    into white, sliding traps . . . ?

How could they know, even stand back and see
The nature of the place they stood on,
When no man can, no man knows where he stands
Until he leaves his place, looks back
            and knows.

Ah, Franklin! I would like to find you
Now, your body spreadeagled like a star,
A human constellation in the snow.
                    The earth insists
There is but one geography, but then
There is another still —
The complex, crushed geography of men.
You carried all maps within you;
Land masses moved in relation to
                    you —
As though you created the Passage
By willing it to be.
                    Ah, Franklin!
To follow you one does not need geography.
At least not totally, but more of that

Instrumental knowledge the bones have,
Their limits, their measurings.
The eye creates the horizon,
The ear invents the wind,
The hand reaching out from a parka sleeve
By touch demands that the touched thing
                    be.

Music and more wind sound effects, fade out

RASMUSSEN:

So I've followed you here
Like a dozen others, looking for relics
            of your ships, your men.
Here to this awful monastery
            where you, where Crozier died,
            and all the men with you died,
Seeking a passage from imagination to
            reality,
Seeking a passage from land to land
            by sea.

Now in the arctic night
I can almost suppose you did not die,
But are somewhere walking between
The icons of ice, pensively
            like a priest,
Wrapped in the cold holiness of snow,
            of your own memory . . .

Music bridge to Franklin, wind sound effects

FRANKLIN:

I brought them here, a hundred and twenty-nine men,
Led them into this bottleneck,
This white asylum.
I chose the wrong channel and
The ice folded in around us,
Gnashing its jaws, folded in
                    around us . . .

The ice clamps and will not open.
For a year it has not opened
Though we bash against it
Like lunatics at padded walls.

My ships, The Terror, The Erebus
Are learning the meanings of their
                    names.
What madman christened them
The ships of Terror and of Hell?
In open sea they did four knots;
Here, they rot and cannot move at all.

Another winter in the ice,
The second one for us, folds in.
Latitude 70 N. November 25,1846.
The sun has vanished.

                Music, etc.

RASMUSSEN:

Nothing then but to sit out the darkness,
The second sterile year,

and wait for spring
And pray the straits would crack
Open, and the dash begin again;
Pray you could drive the ships
Through the yielding, melting floes,
                    drive and press on down
Into the giant virginal strait of
                    Victoria.
But perhaps she might not yield,
She might not let you enter,
                    but might grip
And hold you crushed forever in her stubborn
                    loins,
                    her horrible house,
Her white asylum in an ugly marriage.

Music, etc.

FRANKLIN:

I told him, I told Crozier
The spring is coming, but it's wrong
                    somehow.
Even in summer the ice may not open,
It may not open.
Some of the men have scurvy, Crozier . . .
                    Their faces, the sick ones,
                    their faces reflect their minds.
I can read the disease in their souls.
It's a mildewed chart
On their flesh.
                    But this is no place
To talk of souls; here
The soul becomes the flesh.

Sighs

I may have to send men on foot
To where the passage is,
To prove it, to prove it is there,
That Simpson joins Victoria,
That there is a meaning, a pattern
           imposed on this chaos,
A conjunction of waters,
        a kind of meaning
Even here, even in this place . . .

RASMUSSEN:

A kind of meaning, even here,
Even in this place.
        Yes, yes,
We are men, we demand
That the world be logical, don't we?

But eight of your men went overland
        and saw it, proved it,
Proved the waters found each other
Laughs briefly, bitterly
        as you said,
Saw the one — owing into the other,
Saw the conjunction, the synthesis
        of faith, there
In the white metallic cold.

And returned to tell you, Franklin,
And found you dying in Erebus,
In the hell

of your body,
The last ship of your senses.

June 11, 1847. . .

Music and sound effect bridge

RASMUSSEN:

Crozier took command,
A scientist, understanding magnetism,
                    the pull of elements, but
The laws which attract and as easily repel
Could not pull him from the hell
                    of his science.

Crozier, what laws govern
This final tug of war
                    between life and death,
The human polarities . . . ?
What laws govern these?
                    The ice
Is its own argument.

Music bridge

CROZIER:

It is September, the end of summer . . .

Laughs briefly, bitterly

Summer, there was no summer . . .
Funny how you go on using
            the same old terms
Even when they've lost all meaning.

Two summers, and the ice has not melted.
Has the globe tipped? The axis slipped?
            Is there no sense of season
Anywhere?

September 1847.
We await our *third* winter in the ice.

> *On the word* third *a chilling sound effect*

RASMUSSEN:

But the ice, wasn't it drifting south
Itself, like a ship, a ship within a
Ship?

CROZIER:

The ice is drifting south, but
        not fast enough.
It has time, it has more time than we
        have time;
It has eternity to drift south.
Ice doesn't eat, doesn't get scurvy,
Doesn't die, like my men are dying.

> *Music to suggest a time lapse*

CROZIER:

April 1848. The winter is over.
Supplies to last three months only.
We are leaving the ships for good.

RASMUSSEN:

You went overland, then.
Overland, an ironic word . . .
How can you call this land?
                    It's the white teeth
Of a giant saw,
                    and men crawl through it
Like ants through an upright comb.
Overland. You set out from the ships
In a kind of horrible birth,
                    a forced expulsion
From those two wombs, solid at least,
Three-dimensional, smelling of wood
And metal and familiar things.

Overland . . .

            Music bridge

CROZIER:

April 21,1848. Good Friday.
Our last day in the ships.
We pray, we sing hymns, there
                    is nothing else to do.
We are all of us crucified
                    before an ugly Easter.
Civilization . . . six hundred and seventy miles away.

On the words six hundred and seventy miles
away *more chilling sound effects*

CROZIER:

A hundred and five men left. Three months' supplies.
Our Father who art in heaven,
Hallowed be thy name . . .
                    Six hundred and seventy miles to civilization,
Three months' supplies, a hundred and five men . . .
Give us this day our daily bread
and forgive us . . .
                    scurvy among the men.
                    We leave ship tomorrow.
Thy kingdom come, thy will be done . . . .
                    Six hundred and seventy miles to
                    civilization . . .
For Thine is the kingdom, and the Power,
And the Glory . . .
Our Father
Our Father
Our Father

RASMUSSEN:

April 25, 1848. HMS Terror and
Erebus were deserted, having been beset
since the 12th of September 1846.
The officers and crew consisting of a hundred and five
souls under the command of Captain F. R.
Crozier landed here.
The total loss by deaths in the Expedition
has been to this date nine officers and
fifteen men.

So you pushed on, and sun and snow,
                that marriage of agonizing light
Assailed you.

Music bridge

CROZIER:

In the beginning God made the light
And saw that it was good . . .
                the light . . .
                and saw that it was good . . .

Eerie music

My men fall back, blinded,
                clutching their scorched eyes!
Who ever said that Hell was darkness?
What fool said that light was good
                and darkness evil?
In extremes, all things reverse themselves;
In extremes there are no opposites.

RASMUSSEN:

The naked eye dilates, shrinks,
Goes mad, cannot save itself.
You didn't even have those wooden slits
The eskimos wore
                to censor the sun,
                to select as much light
As the eye can bear.
Some science could have tamed the light
For you,
                not hope, not prayer —
But pairs of simple wooden slits,
Only those, only those ridiculous

                instruments
You need to keep the cosmos out.
I share your irony, Crozier,
That, and your despair . . .

    CROZIER:

        Breathing heavily while speaking

To select what we will and will not see,
To keep the cosmos out with layers of cloth
                and strips of leather —
                That's man, I suppose,
                an arrogant beast. Whether
He is right or wrong is —

O Hell ! Look, Lord, look how
They fall back behind me!

        Music bridge

    CROZIER:

I sent thirty men back to the ships,
Thirty good men back to the Terror, the Erebus
                for food, somehow.
We can go blind but we must eat
                in the white waste.
Though all our senses fall apart
                we must eat
                we must still eat . . .

    RASMUSSEN:

Thirty good men.
On the way back all of them but five

died,
Knelt before the sun for the last time
and died,
Knelt like priests in the whiteness
and died,
on their knees, died,
Or stretched straight out,
Or sitting in a brief stop
which never ended,
died.

It does not matter how.

Five made it back to the ships
And there, in the womb, in the
wooden hulls,
died.
Five who could not go back,
Who could not a second time
Bear the birth, the going out,
the expulsion
into pure worlds of ice.

Music bridge

The men do not return with food.
We push on, we cannot wait here.
The winds wait, the sun waits,
the ice waits, but
We cannot wait here;
to stop is to die
In our tracks,
to freeze like catatonics
In our static houses of bone.

Already we look like statues,
marbled, white.
The flesh and hair bleaches out;
we are cast in plaster.

The ice cannot bear the flesh of men,
The sun will not tolerate coloring;
         we begin already
To move into the ice, to mimic it.
Our Father who art in heaven,
Our Father
Our Father

Music, wind

One night we saw Eskimos
And they were afraid;
They gave us a seal,
They ran away at night . . .

More music, wind

CROZIER:

Slowly

We have come two hundred miles from the ships,
We have come two hundred miles.
There are thirty men left.
It is the end, it is
The end . . .

Wind, bridge to

RASMUSSEN:

Now there was nothing more to do,
        no notes to write and leave in cairns,
        no measurements to take, no
Readings of any temperatures
        save the inner

Agony of the blood.
Now, Crozier, now you come
To the end of science.

CROZIER:

Speaking slowly, painfully

We scattered our instruments behind us,
              and left them where they fell
Like pieces of our bodies, like limbs
We no longer had need for;
              we walked on and dropped them,
              compasses, tins, tools, all of them.
Now we come to the end of science . . .

Now we leave ciphers in the snow,
We leave our instruments in the snow.
It is the end of science.
What magnet do I know of
Which will pull us south . . . ?
              none,
              none but the last inevitable
              one.
Death who draws
Death who reaches out his pulling arms
And draws men in like filings
              on paper.

This is the end of science.
We left it behind us,
A graph in the snow, a horrible cipher,
              a desperate code.
And the sun cannot read, and the snow
              cannot either.

Music, etc. suggesting death

RASMUSSEN:

No, Crozier, the sun cannot read
And the snow cannot either.
But men can, men like me who come
To find your traces, the pieces
Of your pain scattered in the white
                    vaults of the snow.
Men like me who come and stand
                    and learn
The agony your blood learned —
                    how the body is bleached
And the brain itself turns
                    a kind of pure, purged
                    white.

And what happened to the ships —
It hurts to talk of it.
                The Eskimo, Qaqortingneq
Knows —
                let him tell of it . . .

                Wind etc. bridge to Qaqortingneq, who speaks
slowly, falteringly, with language difficulties

QAQORTINGNEQ:

I remember the day
When our fathers found a ship.
They were hunting seals,
And it was spring
And the snow melted around
The holes where the seals breathed . . .

                Music

Far away on the ice
My fathers saw a strange shape,
A black shape, too great to be seals.
They ran home and told all the men
In the village,
And the next day all came to see
This strange thing . . .

It was a ship, and they moved closer,
And saw that it was empty,
That it had slept there for a long time.
My fathers had never seen white men,
And my fathers did not know about ships.
They went aboard the great ship

As though into another world,
Understanding nothing;
They cut the lines of the little boat
Which hung from the ship
And it fell broken to the ice;
They found guns in the ship
And did not understand
And they broke the guns
And used them for harpoons . . .

And they did not understand . . .

They went into the little houses
On the deck of the ship,
And found dead people in beds
Who had lain there a long time.
Then they went down, down
Into the hull of the great ship
And it was dark
And they did not understand the dark . . .

And to make it light they bored a hole
In the side of the ship,
But instead of the light,
The water came in the hole,
And flooded, and sank the ship,
And my fathers ran away,
And they did not understand . . .

Music

RASMUSSEN:

And the papers? Franklin's papers?
The ship's logs, the reports?

QAQORTINGNEQ:

Papers, O yes!

The little children found papers
In the great ship,
But they did not understand papers.
They played with them,
They ripped them up,
They threw them into the wind
Like birds . . .

Music

RASMUSSEN:

Laughing bitterly

Maybe they were right, —
What would papers mean to them?
                cryptic marks, latitudes,
                signatures, journals,
                diaries of despair,
                official reports
Nobody needs to read.
I've seen the real journals
You left us, you Franklin, you Crozier.
I've seen the skulls of your men
                in the snow, their sterile bones
Arranged around cairns like
                compasses,
Marking out all the latitudes
                and longitudes
Of men.

Music

Now the great passage is open,
The one you dreamed of, Franklin,
And great white ships plough through it
Over and over again,
Packed with cargo and carefree men.
It is as though no one had to prove it
Because the passage was always there.
Or . . . is it that the way was invented,
Franklin?
                that you cracked the passage open
With the forces of sheer certainty?
                — or is it that you cannot know,
Can never know,
Where the passage lies
Between conjecture and reality . . . ?

Music, fade out

HELEN

For a short period in the early seventies, Gwendolyn MacEwen, along with her second husband, singer Nikos Tsingos, helped to run *The Trojan Horse*, a coffeehouse, bar and folk-singing establishment on the Danforth, in the Greek section of Toronto. At the same time she was translating, with Tsingos' help, Euripides' *The Trojan Women*, and a number of poems by Yannis Ritsos.

Helen gives the flavor of her translations, which no one reading them could mistake for the work of anyone else. The vocabulary is so much her own that these translations seem almost to have been written by her. It's significant that she would choose to translate *The Trojan Women* and *Helen* - texts filled with the plaint of women, with their powerlessness, victimization and a sense of isolation. Perhaps it was only through translation that she could deal with states of mind she had made such an effort to hold at bay. Or perhaps the growing womens' movement was impinging. For whatever reason, these translations are deeply felt.

Helen, along with *The Trojan Women* and Ritsos' *Orestes*, appeared from Exile Editions in 1981.

HELEN

(Even from a distance the wear and tear showed — crumbling walls with fallen plaster; faded window-shutters; the balcony railings rusted. A curtain stirring outside the window on the upper floor, yellowed, frayed at the bottom. When he approached — hesitantly — he found the same sense of desolation in the garden: disorderly plants, voluptuous leaves, unpruned trees, the odd flower choked in the nettles; the waterless fountains, mouldy; lichen on the beautiful statues. An immobile lizard between the breasts of a young Aphrodite, basking in the last rays of the setting sun. How many years had passed! He was so young then — twenty-two? twenty-three? And she? You could never tell — she radiated so much light, it blinded you; it pierced you through — you couldn't tell anymore what she was, if she was, if you were. He rang the doorbell. Standing in the place he once knew so well, now so strangely changed with its unknown entanglement of dark colors, he heard the sound of the bell ringing, solitary. They were slow to answer the door. Someone peered out from the upper window. It wasn't her. A servant, very young. Apparently laughing. She left the window. Still no answer at the door. Afterwards footsteps were heard inside on the stairway. Someone unlocked the door. He went up. A smell of dust, rotten fruit, dried-up slop, urine. Over here. Bedroom. Wardrobe. Metal mirror. Two tottering carved arm-chairs. A small cheap tin table with coffee cups and cigarette butts. And she? No, no impossible! An old, old woman — one, two hundred years old! But five years ago — Oh no! The bedsheet full of holes. There, unstirring; sitting on the bed; bent over. Only her eyes — larger than ever, autocratic, penetrating, vacant.)

Yes, yes — it's me. Sit down for a while. Nobody comes around
   anymore. I'm starting
to forget how to use words. Anyway, words don't matter. I think
   summer's coming,
the curtains are stirring differently — they're — trying to say somethin
   such stupidities! One of them
has already flown out of the window, straining to break the rings,
to fly over the trees — maybe as well to haul
the whole house away — but the house resists with all corners
and me along with it, despite the fact that I've felt for months
   liberated
from my dead ones, my own self, and this resistance of mine
incomprehensible, beyond my will, strange to me, is all I possess — my
wedlock with this bed, this curtain — is also my fear, as though
my whole body were sustained by the ring with the black stone I
   wear on my forefinger

Now, I examine this stone very closely now in these endless hours
   of night —
it's black, it has no reflections — it grows, it grows, it fills up
with black waters — the waters overflow, swell; I sink,
not to the bottom, but to an upper depth; from up there
I can make out my room down below, myself, the wardrobe, the serva
quibbling voicelessly; I see one of them perched
on a stool and with a hard, spiteful expression,
polishing the photograph of Leda; I see the duster leaving behind
a trail of dust and delicate bubbles which rise and burst
with quiet murmuring all around my ankle-bones or knees.

I notice you also have a perplexed, dumbfounded face, distorted
by the slow undulations of black water — now widening, now
   lengthening your face
with yellow streaks. Your hair's writhing upwards

like an upside down Medusa. But then I say: it's only a stone,
a small precious stone. All the blackness contracts, then
dries up and localizes in the smallest possible knot — I feel it
here, just under my throat. And I'm back again
in my room, on my bed, beside my familiar phials
which stare at me, one by one, nodding — only they can help me
for insomnia, fear, memories, forgetfulness, asthma.

What are you up to? Still in the army? Be careful. Don't
  distress yourself so much
about heroism, honors and glories. What'll you do with them?
  Do you still have
that shield on which you had my face engraved? You were so funny
in your tall helmet with its long tail — so very young,
and shy, as though you'd concealed your handsome face
between the hind legs of a horse whose tail hung all the way down
your bare back. Don't get mad again. Stay awhile longer.

The time of antagonism is over now; desires have dried up;
perhaps now, together, we can observe the same point of futility, where,
  think, the only true encounters are realized — however
  indifferent,
but nonetheless soothing — our new community, bleak, quiet, empty,
without much displacement or opposition — let's just stir the ashes
  of the fireplace,
making now and again long thin lovely burial urns
or sit down on the ground and beat it with soundless palms.

Little by little things lost their meaning, became empty; did
they ever perhaps mean anything? — slack, hollow;
we stuffed them with straw and chaff, to give them form,
let them thicken, solidify, stand firmly — the tables, chairs,

the bed we lay on, the words; always hollow
like the cloth sacks, the vendors' burlap bags;
from the outside you can already make out what's inside them,
potatoes, onions, wheat, corn, almonds, or flour.

Sometimes one of them catches on a nail on the stair
or on the prong of an anchor down in the harbor, it rips open,
the flour spills out — a foolish river. The bag empties itself.
The poor gather up the flour in handfuls to make
some pies or gruel. The bag collapses. Someone
picks it up from its two bottom ends; shakes it out in the air;
a cloud of white dust enfolds him; his hair turns white;
especially his eyebrows turn white. The others watch him.
They don't understand a thing; they wait for him to open his mouth,
     to say something.
He doesn't. He folds up the bag into four sections; he leaves
as he is, white, inexplicable, wordless, as though disguised
as a lewd naked man covered with a sheet,
or like a cunning dead man resurrected in his shroud.

So, events and things don't have any meaning — the same goes for
     words, although
with words we name, more or less, those things we lack, or which
we've never seen — airy, as we say, eternal things —
innocent words, misleading, consoling, equivocal, always
trying to be correct — what a terrible thing,
to have named a shadow, invoking it at night in bed
with the sheet pulled up to your neck, and hearing it, we fools
     think
that we're holding our bodies together, that they're holding us,
     that we're keeping our hold on the world.
Nowadays I forget the names I knew best or get them all mixed up –

Paris, Menelaus, Achilles, Proteus, Theoklymenos, Tefkros,
Castor and Polydeuces — my moralizing brothers; who, I gather
have turned into stars — so they say — pilot-lights for ships —
    Thesus, Pireitheus,
Andromache, Cassandra, Agamemnon — sounds, only formless sounds,
their images unwritten on a window-pane
or a metal mirror or on the shallows of a beach, like that time
on a quiet sunny day, with myriads of masts, after the battle
had abated, and the creaking of the wet ropes on the pulleys
hauled the world up high, like the knot of a sob arrested
in a crystalline throat — you could see it sparkling, trembling
without becoming a scream, and suddenly the entire landscape, the
    ships,
the sailors and the chariots, were sinking into light and anonymity.

Now, another deeper, darker submersion — out of which
some sounds emerge now and then — when hammers were pounding wood
and nailing together a new trireme in a small shipyard; when a huge
four-horse chariot was passing by on the stone road, adding to
    the ticks
from the cathedral clock in another duration, as though
there were more, much more than twelve hours and the horses
were turning around in the clock until they were exhausted; or when
    one night
two handsome young men were singing below my windows
a song for me, without words — one of them one-eyed; the other
wearing a huge buckle on his belt — gleaming in the moonlight.

Words don't come to me on their own now — I search them out as
    though I'm translating
from a language I don't know — nevertheless, I do translate.
    Between the words,

and within them, are deep holes; I peer through them as though
I'm peering through the knots which have fallen from the boards
    of a door
completely closed up, nailed here for ages. I don't see a thing.
No more words or names; I can only single out some sounds — a
    silver candlestick
or a crystal vase rings by itself and all of a sudden stops,
pretending it knows nothing, that it didn't ring, that nobody
struck it, or passed by it. A dress
collapses softly from the chair onto the floor, diverting
attention from the previous sound to the simplicity of nothing.
    However
the idea of a silent conspiracy, although diffused in air,
floats densely higher up, almost immeasurable,
so that you feel the etching of the lines around your mouth grow
    deeper
precisely because of this presence of an intruder who takes over
    your position
turning you into an intruder, right here on your own bed, in your
    own room.

Oh, to be alienated in our very clothes which get old,
in our own skin which gets wrinkled; while our fingers
can no longer grip or even wrap around our bodies
the blanket which rises by itself, disperses, disappears, leaving
    us
bare before the void. Then, the guitar hanging on the wall
with its rusty strings, forgotten for years, begins to quiver
like the jaw of an old woman quivering from cold or fear, and
you have to put your palm flat upon the strings to stop
the contagious chill. But you can't find your hand, you don't
    have one;
and you hear in your guts that it's your own jaw that's shaking.

In this house the air's become heavy and inexplicable, maybe
due to the natural presence of the dead. A trunk opens
on its own, old dresses fall out, rustle, stand up straight
and quietly stroll around; two gold tassels remain on the carpet;
    a curtain
opens — revealing nobody — but they're still there; a cigarette
burns on and off in the ashtray; the person who
left it there is in the other room, rather awkward,
his back turned, gazing at the wall, possibly at a spider
or a damp stain, facing the wall, so the dark
hollow under his protruding cheekbones won't show.

The dead feel no pain for us any more — that's odd, isn't it? —
not so much for them as for us — that neutral intimacy of theirs
within a place which has rejected them and where they don't
    contribute
a thing to the upkeep, nor concern themselves with the run-down
    condition,
them, accomplished and unchangeable, and yet seeming somewhat larger.

This is what sometimes confounds us — the augmentation of the
    unchangeable
and their silent self-sufficiency — not at all haughty; they don't
    try
to force you to remember them, to be pleasing. The women
let their bellies slacken; their stockings sagging, they take
the pins from the silver box; they stick them in the sofa's velvet
one by one, in two straight rows; then pick them up
and begin again with the same polite attention. Someone who's
    very tall
emerges from the hall — he knocks his head against the door;
he doesn't make a single grimace — and neither could the knock be

heard at all.
Yes, they're as foolish as we; only quieter. Another of them
raises his arm ceremoniously, as though to give a blessing to
    someone,
pulls off a piece of the crystal from the chandelier, puts it in his
    mouth
simply, like glass fruit — you think he's going to chew it, to get
    a human function
in motion again — but no; he clenches it between his teeth, thus,
to let the crystal shine with a futile brightness. A woman
takes some face-cream from the little round white jar
with a skilled movement of two of her fingers, and writes
two thick capital letters on the windowpane — they look like L and D —
the sun heats the glass pane, the cream melts, drips down the wall —
and all this means nothing — just two greasy, brief furrows.

I don't know why the dead stay around here without anyone's sympath
    I don't know what they want
wandering around the rooms in their best clothes, their best shoes
polished, immaculate, yet noiselessly as though they never touch
    the floor.
They take up space, sprawl wherever they like, in the two rocking
    chairs,
down on the floor, or in the bathroom; they forget and leave the tap
    dripping;
forget the perfumed bars of soap melting in the water. The servants
passing among them, sweeping with the big broom,
don't notice them. Only sometimes, the laughter of a maid
somewhat confined — it doesn't fly up, out of the window,
it's like a bird tied by the leg with a string, which someone is
    pulling downward.
Then the servants get inexplicably furious with me, they throw the
    broom

here, right into the middle of my room, and go into the kitchen;
    I hear them
making coffee in big briquets, spilling the sugar on the floor —
it crunches under their shoes; the aroma of the coffee
drifts through the hallway, floods the house, observes itself
in the mirror like a silly, dark, impudent face covered with uncombed
    tufts of hair
and two false skyblue earrings, blows its breath on the mirror,
clouds the glass. I feel my tongue probing around in my mouth;
I feel that I've still got some saliva. "A coffee for me too," —
    I call to the servants;
"a coffee," (that's all I ask for; I don't want anything else).
    They
act as though they don't hear. I call over and over again
without bitterness or rage. They don't answer. I hear them
gulping down their coffee from my porcelain cups with the gold brims
and the delicate violet flowers. I become silent and gaze at
that broom flung on the floor like the rigid corpse
of that tall, slim young grocer's boy, who, years ago,
showed me his big phallus between the railings of the garden gate.

Oh yes, I laugh sometimes, and I hear my hoarse laughter rise up,
no longer from the chest, but much deeper, from the feet; even
    deeper,
from the earth. I laugh. How pointless it all was,
how purposeless, ephemeral and insubstantial — riches, wars, glories,
jealousies, jewels, my own beauty.
    What foolish legends,
swans and Troys and loves and brave deeds.
    I met my old
lovers again in mournful night feasts, with white beards,
with white hair, with bulging bellies, as though they were
already pregnant with their death, devouring with a strange craving

the roasted goats, without looking into a shoulder-blade — what
   should they look for? —
a level shadow filled all of it with a few white specks.
I, as you know, preserved my former beauty
as if by miracle (but also with tints, herbs and salves,
lemon juice and cucumber water). I was only terrified to see
   in their faces
the passing also of my own years. At that time I was tightening
   my belly muscles,
I was tightening my cheeks with a false smile, as though
propping up two crumbling walls with a thin beam.

That's how I was, shut in, confined, strained — God, what exhaustion
confined every moment (even in my sleep) as though I were inside
freezing armor or a wooden corset around my whole body, or with
my own Trojan Horse, deceptive and narrow, knowing even then
the pointlessness of deceit and self-deception, the pointlessness of
   fame,
the pointlessness and temporality of every victory.
                        A few months ago,
when I lost my husband (was it months or years?), I left
my Trojan Horse forever down in the stable, with his old horses,
so the scorpions and spiders could circle around inside him. I
   don't tint my hair anymore.

Huge warts have sprouted on my face. Thick hairs have grown
   around my mouth —
I clutch them, I don't look at myself in the mirror —
long, wild hairs — as though someone else has enthroned himself
   within me,
an impudent, malevolent man, and it's his beard
that emerges from my skin. I leave him be — what can I do? —
I'm afraid that if I chased him away, he'd drag me along behind hir

on't go away. Stay awhile longer. I haven't talked for ages.
obody comes to see me anymore. They were all in a hurry to leave,
aw it in their eyes — all in a hurry for me to die. Time doesn't
roll on.

e servants loathe me. I hear them opening my drawers at night
king the lacy things, the jewels, the gold coins; who can tell
they'll leave me with a single decent dress for some necessary
hour
a single pair of shoes. They even took my keys
om under my pillow; I didn't stir at all; I pretended I was
asleep —
ey would have taken them one day anyway — I don't want them to know
at least, that I know.

hat would I do without even them? "Patience, patience," I tell
myself;
atience" — and this too is the smallest form of victory,
hen they read the old letters of my admirers
the poems great poets dedicated to me; they read them
ith idiotic bombast and many mistakes in pronunciation,
accentuation, metre
d syllabification — I don't correct them. I pretend I don't hear.
Occasionally
ey draw big moustaches with my black eyebrow pencil
my statues, or stick an ancient helmet or a chamber-pot
their heads. I regard them coolly. They get angry.

ne day, when I felt a little better, I asked them again
make up my face. They did. I asked for a mirror.
ey had painted my face green, with a black mouth. "Thank you,"
I told them,
though I hadn't seen anything strange. They were laughing. One
of them

stripped right in front of me, put on my gold veils, and like that,
bare-legged with her thick legs began to dance,
leapt upon the table — frenzied; danced and danced, bowing
in imitation, as it were, of my old gestures. High up on her thigh
she had a love-bite from a man's strong even teeth.
I watched them as though I were in the theatre — with no humiliati
   or grief,
or indignation — for what purpose? — But I kept telling myself:
"one day we'll die," or rather: "one day you will," and that
was a sure revenge, fear and consolation. I looked
everything straight in the eye with an indescribable, apathetic
   clarity, as if
my eyes were independent of me; I looked at my own eyes
situated a metre away from my face, like the panes
of a window far removed, from behind which someone else
sits and observes the goings-on in an unknown street
with closed coffee, photograph and perfume shops,
and I had the feeling that a beautiful crystal phial
broke, and the perfume spilled out in the dusty showcase. Everyon
   passing,
pausing vaguely, sniffing the air, remembered something good
and then disappeared behind the pepper-trees or at the end of the
   street.

Now and again, I can still sense that aroma — I mean, I remember
isn't it strange? — those things we usually consider great, dissolve,
   fade away —
Agamemnon's murder, the slaughter of Clytemnestra (they'd sent
one of her beautiful necklaces from Mycenae, made
from small gold masks, held together by links
from the upper tips of their ears — I never wore it). They're
   forgotten;
some other things remain, unimportant, meaningless things; I

recall seeing one day
a bird perching on a horse's back; and that baffling thing
seemed to explain (especially for me) a certain beautiful mystery.

I still remember, as a child, on the banks of the Eurotus, beside
    the burning leanders,
the sound of a tree peeling off alone; the bark
falling gently into the water and floating away like triremes,
and I waited, stubbornly, for a black butterfly with orange stripes
to land on a piece of bark, amazed that although it was immobile,
    it moved,
and this broke me up, that butterflies, although adept in air,
know nothing about travelling in water, or rowing. And it came.

There are certain strange, isolated moments, almost funny. A man
takes a stroll at midday wearing a huge hamper on his head; the
    basket
hides his whole face as though he were headless or disguised
by an enormous eyeless, multi-eyed head. Another man,
strolling along, musing in the dusk, stumbles over something,
    curses,
turns back, searches — finds a pebble, picks it up; kisses it; then
remembers to look around; goes off guiltily. A woman
slips her hand inside her pocket; finds nothing; takes her hand
    out,
raises it and carefully scrutinizes it, as though it were breathed
    on by the powder of emptiness.

A waiter's caught a fly in his hand — he doesn't crush it;
a customer calls him; he's absorbed; he loosens his fist; the fly
escapes and lands on the glass. A piece of paper rolls down the
    street

hesitantly, spasmodically, attracting nobody's
attention — enjoying it all. But yet, every so often
it gives off a certain crackle which belies it; as though looking for
an impartial witness to its humble, secret route. And all these thing
have a desolate and inexplicable beauty, and a profound pain
because of our own odd and unknown gestures — don't they?

The rest is lost as though it were nothing. Argos, Athens, Sparta,
Corinth, Thebes, Sikion — shadows of names. I utter them; they
    re-echo as though they're sinking
into the incomplete. A well-bred, lost dog stands
in front of the window of a cheap dairy. A young girl passing by
    looks at it;
it doesn't respond; its shadow spreads wide in the sidewalk.
I never learned the reason. I doubt it even exists. There's
    only
this humiliating compulsive (by whom?) approval
as we nod "yes," as though greeting someone
with incredible servility, though nobody's passing, nobody's there.

I think another person, with a totally colorless voice related to me
    one evening
the details of my life; I was sleepy and wishing deep inside
that he'd finally stop; that I could close my eyes,
and sleep. And as he spoke, in order to do something, to fight
    off sleep,
I counted the tassels on my shawl, one by one, to the tune of
a silly children's song of Blindman's Bluff, until
the meaning got lost in the repetition. But the sound remains —
noises, thuds, scrapings — the drone of silence, a discordant wee
ing,
someone scratches the wall with his fingernails, a scissor falls
    onto the floor boards,
someone coughs — his hand over his mouth, so as not to awaken t

other
sleeping with him — maybe his death — stops; and once again
that spiralling drone from an empty, shut-up well.

At night I hear the servants moving my big pieces of furniture;
they take them down the stairs — a mirror, held like a stretcher,
reveals the worn-out plaster designs on the ceiling; a windowpane
knocks against the railings — it doesn't break; the old overcoat on
     the coat-rack
raises its empty arms for a moment, slips them back into the pockets;
the little wheels of the sofa's legs creak on the floor. I can feel
right here on my elbow the scratching on the wall made by the corners
     of the wardrobe
or the big carved table. What are they going to do with them?
     "Goodbye," I say
almost mechanically, as though bidding farewell to a visitor who's
     always a stranger. There's only
that vague droning which lingers in the hallway as though from the
     horn
of downfallen hunting lords in the last drops of rain, in a burnt-out
     forest.
Honestly, so many useless things collected with so much greed
blocked the space — we couldn't move; our knees
knocked against wooden, stony, metallic knees. Oh, we've really
got to grow old, very old, to become just, to reach that
mild impartiality, that sweet lack of interest in comparisons,
     judgements,
when it's no longer our lot to take part in anything except this
     quietness.

Oh yes, how many silly battles, heroic deeds, ambitions, arrogance,
sacrifices and defeats, defeats, and still more battles for things
that others determined when we weren't there. Innocent people
poking hairpins into their eyes, banging their heads
on the high wall, knowing full well that it wouldn't fall
or even crack, just to see at least from a little crevice

a slight sky-blue unshadowed by time and their own shadows.
Meanwhile — who knows —
perhaps there, where someone is resisting, hopelessly, perhaps there
human history begins, so to speak, and man's beauty
among rusty bits of iron and the bones of bulls and horses,
among ancient tripods where some laurel still burns
and the smoke rises curling in the sunset like a golden fleece.

Stay awhile longer. Evening's falling. The golden fleece we spoke
    of — Oh, thought
comes slowly to us women — it relaxes somehow. On the other hand
    men
never stop to think — maybe they're afraid; maybe they don't want
to look their fear straight in the eye, to see their fatigue, to
    relax —
timid, conceited, busybodies, they surge into darkness. Their
    clothes
always smell of smoke from a conflagration they've passed by or
    through
unwittingly. Quickly they undress; fling
their clothes onto the floor; fall into bed. But even their bodies
reek of smoke — it numbs them. I used to find, when they were final
    asleep,
some fine burnt leaves among the hairs on their chests
or some ash-grey down from slain birds. Then
I'd gather them up and keep them in a small box — the only signs
of a secret communion — I never showed these to them — they wouldr
    have recognized them.

Sometimes, oh yes, they were beautiful — naked as they were,
surrendered to sleep,
thoroughly unresisting, loosened up, their big strong bodies,
damp and softened, like roaring rivers surging down

from high mountains into a quiet plain, or like abandoned children.
    At such times
I really loved them, as though I'd given birth to them. I noticed
    their long eyelashes
and I wanted to draw them back into me, to protect them, or in
    this way
to couple with their whole bodies. They were sleeping. And sleep
    demands respect
from you, because it's so rare. That's all over too. All forgotten.

Not that I don't remember anymore — I do; it's just that the memories
are no longer emotional — they can't move us — they're impersonal,
    placid,
clear right into their most bloody corners. Only one of them
still retains some air around it, and breathes.

                                    That late afternoon,
when I was surrounded by the endless shrieks of the wounded,
the mumbled curses of the old men and their wonder of me, amid
the smell of overall death, which, from time to time glittered
on a shield or the tip of a spear or the metope
of a neglected temple or the wheel of a chariot — I went up alone
onto the high walls and strolled around.

                                    Alone, utterly alone, between
the Trojans and Achaeans, feeling the wind pressing my fine veils
against me, brushing my nipples, embracing my whole body
both clothed and naked, with only a single wide silver belt
holding my breasts up high —

                        there I was, beautiful, untouched, experienced
while my two rivals in love were duelling and the fate of the long war
was being determined —

                    I didn't even see the strap of Paris' helmet
severed — instead I saw a brightness from its brass,
a circular brightness, as his opponent swung it in rage
around his head — an illumined zero.

It wasn't really worth looking at —
the will of the gods had shaped things from the start; and Paris,
divested of his dusty sandals, would soon be in bed,
cleansed by the hands of the goddess, waiting for me, smirking,
pretentiously hiding a false scar on his side with a pink bandage.
I didn't watch anymore; hardly even listened to their war-cries —
I, high up on the walls, over the heads of mortals, airy, carnate,
belonging to no one, needing no one
as though I were (I, independent) absolute Love — free
from the fear of death and time, with a white flower in my hair,
with a flower between my breasts, and another in between my lips
    hiding for me
the smile of freedom.

They could have shot
their arrows at me from either side.

I was an easy target
walking slowly on the walls, completely etched
against the golden crimson of the evening sky.

I kept my eyes closed
to make any hostile gesture easy for them — knowing deeply
that none of them would dare. Their hands trembled with awe
at my beauty and immortality —

(maybe I can elaborate on that:
I didn't fear death because I felt it was so far from me).

Then
I tossed down the two flowers from my hair and breasts — keeping
    the third one
in my mouth — I tossed them down from both sides of the wall
with an absolutely impartial gesture.

Then the men, both within and withou
threw themselves upon each other, enemies and friends, to snatch
the flowers, to offer them to me — my own flowers. I didn't see
anything else after that — only bent backs, as if all of them
were kneeling on the ground, where the sun was drying the blood –
    maybe

they had even crushed the flowers.
                                        I didn't see.
                                                    I'd raised my arms
and risen on the tips of my toes, and ascended
letting the third flower also drop from my lips.
All this remains with me still — a sort of consolation, a remote
    justification, and perhaps
this will remain, I hope, somewhere in the world — a momentary freedom,
illusory too of course — a game of our luck and our ignorance. In
    precisely
that position (as I recall), the sculptors worked on
my last statues; they're still out there in the garden;
you must have seen them when you came in. Sometimes I also (when
    the servants are in good spirits
and hold me by my arms to take me to that chair
in front of the window), I also can see them. They glow in the sun-
    light. A white heat
wafts from the marble right up here. I won't dwell on it any
    longer.
It tires me out too after awhile. I'd rather watch a part of the
    street
where two or three kids play with a rag ball, or some girl
lowers a basket on a rope from the balcony across the way.
Sometimes the servants forget I'm there. They don't come to put
    me back in bed.
I stay all night gazing at an old bicycle, propped up
in front of the lit window of a new candy store,
until the lights go out, or I fall asleep on the window-sill.
    Every now
and then I think that a star wakes me, falling through space
like the saliva from a toothless, slack mouth of an old man.
                                                            Now
it's been ages since they've taken me to the window. I stay here in
    bed

sitting up or lying down — I can handle that. To pass the time
I grasp my face — an unfamiliar face — touch it, feel it, count
the hairs, the wrinkles, the warts — who's inside
this face?

       Something acrid rises in my throat — nausea and fear,
a silly fear, my God, that even the nausea might be lost. Stay
   for awhile —
a little light's coming through the window — they must have lit the
   street lamps.

Wouldn't you like me to ring for something for you? — some
   preserved cherries
or candied bitter orange — maybe something's left in the big jars,
turned to congealed sugar by now — if, of course the greedy servar
have left anything. The last few years I've been busy
making sweets — what else is there to do?

                      After Troy — life in Sparta
was very dull — really provincial; shut up all day at home,
among the crowded spoils of so many wars; and memories,
faded and annoying, sneaking up behind you in the mirror
as you combed your hair, or in the kitchen emerging
from the greasy vapors of the pot; and you hear in the water's
   boiling
a few dactylic hexameters from the Third Rhapsody
as a cock crows discordantly, close by, from a neighbor's coop.

You surely know how humdrum our life is. Even the newspapers
have the same shape, size, headlines — I no longer read them.
   Over and over
flags on balconies, national celebrations, parades
of toy soldiers — only the cavalry maintained something improvise
something personal — maybe because of the horses. The dust rose
   like a cloud;

we closed the window — afterward you'd have to go about dusting, piece by piece,
vases, little boxes, picture frames, small porcelain statues, mirrors, buffets.
I stopped going to the celebrations. My husband used to come back sweating,
fling himself on his food, licking his chops, re-chewing
old, boring glories and resentments gone up in smoke. I stared at
his waistcoat buttons which were about to pop — he'd become quite fat.
Under his chin a large black stain flickered.

Then I'd prop my chin up, distractedly, continuing my meal,
feeling my lower jaw move in my hand
as though it were detached from my head, and I was holding it naked in my palm.
Maybe because of this I got fat too. I don't know. Everybody seemed scared —
I saw them sometimes from the windows — walking on a slant,
sort of limping, as though they were concealing something under their arms. Afternoons
the bells rang dismally. The beggars knocked on the doors. In the distance
as night fell, the white-washed facade of the Maternity Hospital seemed whiter,
farther away and unknowable. We lit the lamps quickly. I'd alter
an old dress. Then the sewing machine broke down; they took it
into the basement with those old romantic oil paintings
full of banal mythical scenes — Aphrodites rising from the sea, Eagles and Ganymedes.

One by one our old acquaintances left. The mail diminished.
Only a brief postcard for special occasions, birthdays —

a stereotyped scene of Mount Taygetos with ridged peaks, very blue
a part of the Eurotas river with white pebbles and rhododendrons,
or the ruins of Mistras with wild fig trees. But more often,
telegrams of condolences. No answers came. Maybe
the recipient had died in the meantime — we don't get news anymo
My husband travelled no more. Didn't open a book. In his later
     years
he grew very nervous. He smoked incessantly. Strolled around at
     nights
in the huge living room, with those tattered brown slippers
and his long nightgown. At noon, at the table, he'd bring up
     memories
of Clytemnestra's infidelity and how right Orestes' actions were
as though he were threatening someone. Who cared? I didn't even
     listen. Yet
when he died, I missed him much — I missed most of all his silly
     threats,
as though they'd frozen me into an immobile position in time,
as though they'd prevented me from becoming old.
                                        Then I used to dream
of Odysseus, he too with the same agelessness, with his smart
     triangular cap,
delaying his return, that crafty guy — with the pretense of imaginary
     dangers,
whereas he'd throw himself (supposedly ship-wrecked) at times in
     the arms of a Circe, at times in the arms
of a Nausicaa, to have the barnacles taken off his chest, to be
     bathed
with small bars of rose soap, to have the scar on his knee kissed,
     to be anointed with oil.

I think he also reached Ithaca — dull, fat Penelope must have muffled
     him up
in those things she weaves. I never got a message from him since
     then —

the servants might have torn them up — what does it matter any-
more?
The Symblygades
shifted to another more inner place — you can feel them
immobile, softened — worse than ever — they don't crush,
they drown you in a thick, black fluid — nobody escapes them.
You may go now. Night's fallen. I'm sleepy. Oh, to close my eyes,
to sleep, to see nothing outside or inside, to forget
the fear of sleeping and awakening. I can't. I jump up —
I'm afraid I'll never wake again. I stay up, listening to the snoring
of the servants from the living room, the spiders on the walls,
the cockroaches in the kitchen, the dead snoring
with deep inhalations, as though sound asleep, calmed down.
Now I'm even losing my dead. I've lost them. They're gone.

Sometimes, after midnight, the rhythmic hoofbeats of the horses
of a late carriage can be heard, as though they are returning
from a dismal show of some broken-down theatre in the
neighborhood with its plaster fallen from the ceiling, its peeling walls,
its enormous faded red curtain drawn,
shrunken from too many washings, leaving a space below
to reveal the bare feet of the great stage manager or the electrician
maybe rolling up a paper forest so the lights can be shut off.

That crack is still alight, while in the auditorium
the applause and the chandeliers are long since vanished. The air
is heavy with the breath of silence, the hum of silence beneath
the empty seats together with the shells from sunflower seeds and
    twisted-up tickets,
a few buttons, a lace handkerchief, and a piece of red string.

. . . And that scene, on the walls of Troy — did I really undergo an
    ascension,

letting fall from my lips — ? Sometimes even now,
as I lie here in bed, I try to raise my arms, to stand
on tiptoe — to stand on air — the third flower —

(She stopped talking. Her head fell back. She might
have been asleep. The other person got up. He didn't say
good-night. Darkness had already come. As he went out into
the corridor, he felt the servants glued to the wall, eavesdrop-
ping. Motionless. He went down the stairs as though into a
deep well, with the feeling that he wouldn't find any exit —
any door. His fingers, contracted, searched for the doorknob.
He even imagined that his hands were two birds gasping for
want of air, yet knowing at the same time that this was no
more than the expression of self-pity which we usually com-
pare with vague fear. Suddenly voices were heard from
upstairs. The electric lights were turned on in the corridor, on
the stairs, in the rooms. He went up again. Now he was sure.
The woman was sitting on the bed with her elbow propped
up on the tin table, her cheek resting in her palm. The ser-
vants were noisily going in and out. Somebody was making a
phone call in the hall. The women in the neighborhood
rushed in. "Ah, ah," they cried, as they hid things under their
dresses. Another phone call. Already the police were coming
up. They sent the servants and the women away, but the
neighbors had time to grab the bird cages with the canaries,
some flower pots with exotic plants, a transistor, an electric
heater. One of them grabbed a gold picture frame. They put
the dead woman onto a stretcher. The person in charge sealed
up the house — "until the rightful owners are found," he said
— although he knew there weren't any. The house would

stay like that, sealed up for forty days, and after, its possessions — as many as were saved — would be auctioned off for the public good. "To the morgue," he said to the driver. The covered car went off. Everything suddenly disappeared. Total silence. He was alone. He turned and looked around. The moon had risen. The statues in the garden were dimly lit — her statues, solitary, beside the trees, outside of the closed house. And a silent, deceitful moon. Where could he go now?)

May-August, 1970

From *THE SHADOW-MAKER*
and *THE ARMIES OF THE MOON*

The Shadow-Maker was published in 1969 by Macmillan, and won the Governor-General's Award. *The Armies of the Moon* was also published by Macmillan, in 1972. This was a prolific period for her: two books of poetry and two substantial prose works — the novel, *King of Egypt, King of Dreams,* and *Noman,* a collection of stories — were published within four years.

In several of these poems, MacEwen turns away from her more usual geography and source of metaphors, the Middle East, and uses instead — as in *Terror and Erebus* — that of her native country. She was simultaneously exploring this territory in prose, in the collection of stories which appeared in 1972, *Noman.* *The Armies of the Moon* contains all of *The Nine Arcana of the Kings,* which had been published piecemeal in earlier books and magazines. This sequence is strongly connected with the writing of her long historical novel about the Egyptian king Akhnaton, *King of Egypt, King of Dreams,* which was published in 1971. Like Sylvia Plath, MacEwen kept hoping that she would be able to make a living through more commercially viable forms, but this never happened. ·

The nocturnal qualities of both these titles indicate the direction MacEwen's poetry was taking as the sixties ended and the seventies began: down rather than up, away from the exuberant fire and sparkle of her earlier poetry and towards a more taciturn, more introspective, and darker probing of the shadow side — the destructive but necessary "left hand" of nature and of the self — that had been present in her work from the beginning.

There is something down there and you want it told.

THE RED BIRD YOU WAIT FOR

You are waiting for someone to confirm it,
You are waiting for someone to say it plain,
Now we are here and because we are short of time
I will say it; I might even speak its name.

It is moving above me, it is burning my heart out,
I have felt it crash through my flesh,
I have spoken to it in a foreign tongue,
I have stroked its neck in the night like a wish.

Its name is the name you have buried in your blood,
Its shape is a gorgeous cast-off velvet cape,
Its eyes are the eyes of your most forbidden lover
And its claws, I tell you its claws are gloved in fire.

You are waiting to hear its name spoken,
You have asked me a thousand times to speak it,
You who have hidden it, cast it off, killed it,
Loved it to death and sung your songs over it.

The red bird you wait for falls with giant wings —
A velvet cape whose royal color calls us kings
Is the form it takes, uninvited, it descends,
It is the Power and the Glory forever, Amen.

POEM

It is not lost, it is moving forward always,
Shrewd, and huge as thunder, equally dark.
Soft paws kiss its continents, it walks
Between lava avenues, it does not tire.

It is not lost, tell me how can you lose it?
Can you lose the shadow which stalks the sun?
It feeds on mountains, it feeds on seas,
It loves you most when you are most alone.

Do not deny it, do not blaspheme it,
Do not light matches on the dark of its shores.
It will breathe you out, it will recede from you.
What is here, what is with you now, is yours.

THE DISCOVERY

do not imagine that the exploration
ends, that she has yielded all her mystery
or that the map you hold
cancels further discovery

I tell you her uncovering takes years,
takes centuries, and when you find her naked
look again,
admit there is something else you cannot name,
a veil, a coating just above the flesh
which you cannot remove by your mere wish

when you see the land naked, look again
(burn your maps, that is not what I mean),
I mean the moment when it seems most plain
is the moment when you must begin again

THE PORTAGE

We have travelled far with ourselves
and our names have lengthened;
      we have carried ourselves
on our backs, like canoes
in a strange portage, over trails,
insinuating leaves
and trees dethroned like kings,
      from water-route to
      water-route
seeking the edge, the end,
the coastlines of this land.

On earlier journeys we
were master ocean-goers
going out, and evening always found us
spooning the ocean from our boat,
      and gulls, undiplomatic
      couriers brought us
cryptic messages from shore
till finally we sealords vowed
we'd sail no more.

Now under a numb sky, somber
cumuli weigh us down;
the trees are combed for winter
and bears' tongues have melted
all the honey;
      there is a loud
suggestion of thunder;
subtle drums under

the candid hands of Indians
are trying to tell us
why we have come.

But now we fear movement
and now we dread stillness;
we suspect it was the land
that always moved, not our ships;
we are in sympathy with the fallen
trees; we cannot relate
      the causes of our grief.
We can no more carry
our boats our selves
over these insinuating trails.

DARK PINES UNDER WATER

This land like a mirror turns you inward
And you become a forest in a furtive lake;
The dark pines of your mind reach downward,
You dream in the green of your time,
Your memory is a row of sinking pines.

Explorer, you tell yourself this is not what you came for
Although it is good here, and green.
You had meant to move with a kind of largeness,
You had planned a heavy grace, an anguished dream.

But the dark pines of your mind dip deeper
And you are sinking, sinking, sleeper
In an elementary world;
There is something down there and you want it told.

THE SHADOW-MAKER

I have come to possess your darkness, only this.

My legs surround your black, wrestle it
As the flames of day wrestle night
And everywhere you paint the necessary shadows
On my flesh and darken the fibers of my nerve;
Without these shadows I would be
In air one wave of ruinous light
And night with many mouths would close
Around my infinite and sterile curve.

Shadow-maker create me everywhere
Dark spaces (your face is my chosen abyss),
For I said I have come to possess your darkness,
Only this.

THE RETURN

I gave you many names and masks
And longed for you in a hundred forms
And I was warned the masks would fall
And the forms would lose their fame
And I would be left with an empty name

(For that was the way the world went,
For that was the way it had to be,
To grow, and in growing lose you utterly)

But grown, I inherit you, and you
Renew your first and final form in me,
And though some masks have fallen
And many names have vanished back into my pen
Your face bears the birth-marks I recognize in time
You stand before me now, unchanged

(For this is the way it has to be;
To perceive you is an act of faith
Though it is you who have inherited me)

THE CHILD DANCING

there's no way I'm going to write about
the child dancing in the Warsaw ghetto
in his body of rags

there were only two corpses
on the pavement that day
and the child I will not write about
had a face as pale and trusting
as the moon

(so did
the boy with a green belly full of dirt
lying by the roadside
in a novel of Kazantzakis
and the small girl T. E. Lawrence wrote about
who they found after the Turkish massacre
with one shoulder chopped off, crying:
"Don't hurt me, Baba!")

I don't feel like slandering them with poetry.

the child who danced
in the Warsaw ghetto
to some music no one else could hear
had moon-eyes, no
green horror and no fear
but something worse

a simple desire to please
the people who stayed
to watch him shuffle back and forth,
his feet wrapped in the newspapers
of another ordinary day

A DANCE AT THE MENTAL HOSPITAL

the imponderable agony
of being here, not just
in the dusty auditorium
smelling of drugs and lemonade
but in the world, alive,
and conscious, and alone
is what makes the dance so
strange.
(we are aware
someone has put us here,
no one was really invited.)
the steps will knit together
some wide wound
that life has made. some wear
the furious defiant face
of a baby first forced to breathe;
others, from behind the slow glazed
smiles try valiantly to please.
still others stare
and cast wild eyes upon this gathering.

I think of the tale about the madman who believed all
the horrors of the world were committed to a single rose in the
hospital garden, and who struggled night after night to
get out and destroy the rose, and finally did, with his
hands bloody from the bars. He was good and mad as Christ,
and held the evil rose against his chest until he and it
both died at dawn.
the imponderable agony
of being here, of having

to have a shape, a foot, an ugly face,
a mind, a fit upon the floor
when the soul breaks out of the screeching teeth
and every nerve and muscle is screaming for release
but now they are dancing, ah, slow as a nightmare
dances in the night across stale beds
beneath impossible stars (will there
be secret trysts tonight upon the sour stairs?)

I too must clutch the world's most beautiful and evil rose
against my chest and stare,
and cast wild eyes upon this gathering.

JEWELLERY

I wear it more to be its captive
than to captivate; I want
to be the prisoner of gold,
to hear my voice break through
the chain which holds my song
in check, or watch the tendons
flicker under
the band about my wrist
which makes my gestures
conscious and restrained;
the circular earrings
familiar as my name
have tamed my mind
as the single ring
has tamed my hand.

You have made a glittering prison
of all my jewellery,
you knew I never wanted
to be free.

HYPNOS

He lies there in a wilderness of sheets
and his body inhabits strange spaces, oblique
dimensions;
             like the keen emptiness of a child's eye
             it offers me no entry and no alibi.
Horses (I think) charge into
the white night of his sleep.
He celebrates the birthdays of his dreams
and does not know I ponder
how I might join him there.

Yet I fear to even if I could
for in his sleep he is powerful
as a withheld word.

He lies there accomplished and unknown,
his limbs arranged by passion and by art,
a fluid beauty he inhabits all alone.
The dark bird of war is dormant in his loins
and prophets reside in the seeds of his kiss;
             the generations of his mouth are legion
             yet his body is inviolably his.

He may lie, he may live there forever
and I can say nothing of the meaning of this sleeper.

ARCANUM ONE: THE PRINCE

and in the morning the king loved you most
and wrote your name with a sun and a beetle
and a crooked ankh, and in the morning
you wore gold mainly, and the king adorned you
with many more names.

beside fountains, both of you slender
as women, circled and walked together
like sunrays circling water, both of you
slender as women wrote your names with
beetles and with suns, and spoke together
in the golden mornings.

and the king entered your body
into the bracelet of his name
and you became a living syllable
in his golden script, and your body
escaped from me like founting water
all the daylong.

but in the evenings you wrote my name
with a beetle and a moon, and lay upon me
like a long broken necklace which had fallen
from my throat, and the king loved you
most in the morning, and his glamorous love
lay lengthwise along us all the evening.

ARCANUM TWO: THE CONSPIRATOR

my brother, you board the narrow boat and the river owns you
over and over; why do you sail like this between your sister
and the distant king? my chamber is full of politics
and hunger. why do you go to him? his chin is thin
and his thighs bulge. why do you go to the king your father?

your boat, your narrow boat goes forth each morning
and snouts of crocodiles worry the water.
why do you go each morning after
our bodies make narrow rivers together?

I know how you plot against the king your father
whose thighs flung you forth as from a salty river;
you will steal the crown which bulges from his head
and mount the thin throne which no one holds forever.

O do not go to the king our father
but stay in this house beside the worried river;
there are a thousand kingdoms yet to conquer
in the narrow nights when we lie together,
and the distant king on his thin and hungry throne
can neither live nor lie nor sing forever.

ARCANUM THREE: THE DEATH OF THE PRINCE

He was employed upon the marble floor
Between the fountain and the pillars.
    They looked for him, the silvery guards
    Sought him all daylong, and my brother
Did not hear them calling through the halls.

And finding him employed upon the marble floor
They fell before him crying: Majesty!
    (Lord, his mouth was terrible
    And his cheek a granite cliff)
And he lifted up his head and smiled.

He was destroyed upon the marble floor
Between the fountain and the pillars
    And I bent over him to call his name,
    His secret name whose syllables were thunder —
Then I took the heavy crown and threw it in the river.

ARCANUM FOUR: THE EMBALMING

along your body strips of gold unroll
your name which caused a kingdom's fall
and your wrapped ribs, my silent one,
refuse the sun, and down your legs run
legends of the night. in white cloth I wound you
in your final house beside the water
and I know the gates are locked forever,
the gates of light are locked forever
as my loins lock, as the river.

in white cloth bound, and blind
you breathe in death the winds of night
as the sweet stiff corpse of your petrified
sex points upward into heaven
in your tomb beside the river,
though the gates of light are locked forever,
the legs and lips of light are locked forever.

my fingers twice have traced
your name all down your flesh, and they
have dipped its signs in water.
now sleep my blind, my silent brother
as my womb locks, as the river,
your tomb a virgin by jackals sealed
and the gates of light are locked forever.

ARCANUM FIVE: THE PRAYER

death is a snake on your smashed brow
but still I beg you to get up and go
beyond the drowning river where your crown lies
towards the sighing house of reeds where I
stand waiting in the hollow doorway of eternity.

O brother, from your tomb arise! your bones
are targets in a hunter's eyes, your soul
the naked arrow which he fires.

in the name of our father, by the ring he wore,
come touch this floor with feet that burned
a thousand times the grass between the river
and this fervent house.
as bird arise, as arrow! and tomorrow
let the strips of linen fall.
all your limbs are tombs of sorrow.
I beg you now, my silent brother
to crash those gates which are not locked forever.
O bless and break them ten times over!

ARCANUM SIX: THE CENTURIES

I waited two millennia in the house beside the river
calling to the north wind many times over,
and feeding doves, and laying fruit beside your tomb
which thieves and beggars stole by night in summer,
and burning prayers and perfume on the hungry altar.
elsewhere slept our mad forgotten father
and the land fell into wretchedness, and later
watersnakes and foreign boats profaned the river.

and sometimes you visited as bird the thirsty bed
where we had lain, and hovered above and said,
"I will come back in better forms than this,
my sister, but the gates are hard to break,
so hard to break you cannot know
and death is like the long sleep after love
when nothing can persuade the limbs to move."

your tired wings were songs among the leaves
and on my thighs you left your shining, unreal seed.

and other centuries I do not try to count
with doves and thieves and moons appeared and went,
with stars that wrote strange warnings in the skies.
the eyes of many kingdoms closed, the palace was defiled
by princes with strange-colored eyes.

brother, I awaited the end of all the world.

ARCANUM SEVEN: THE RETURN

now as I wear around my neck a necklace
of a million suns, you come
undead, unborn, thou Ghost of the morning!

I notice that you wear our father's ring
but I must say no more
for the bed of ebony and straw
lies like a fallen song upon the floor
where last we left it, broken with love and bare.
the world will loathe our love of salt and fire
and none will let you call me sister here.

see how my body bears the mouthmarks made
in times long past, star-wounds in night unhealed;
since then it was a cave by jackals sealed.
but now my legs are once more cages
for a great far-flying bird, my breasts
small pyramids of love, my mouth
is empty of the dark wine of my waiting.

O tell me all the things you saw,
and call me sister,
and bless this bed of ebony and straw.

ARCANUM EIGHT: THE STORY

"sister, from the gates and fields of night I came
lured by your voice as it spoke my name
over water and fire, and the voice of him
who told me that his sun would burn forever.

"I'll tell you why I went each morning to the river
and sailed towards that old man on the throne.
his seed struggled in my reluctant thighs
and the ring on his hand was stone
and his eyes were the mirrors of the world
and he was the very lord of gold.

"so I went each morning to the king my father.
but all is told, I cannot tell another thing
about how his blood was the birth of my soul
and how with my own hands I killed the king, the king.

"now when the sun is born each day at dawn
I will lie along your body as a boat along a river
and place my soul a blazing ornament upon your breasts
and burn with my bones my name all down your flesh.
sister, by a dark love bound and blind
I touch you now, in this forbidden time
and my white robes of death unwind."

ARCANUM NINE: THE RING

I do not adorn you with any more names
for the living ghost of the king our father
hovers forever above our secret bed
like the royal hawk with wings outspread
on whose head the awful sun burns out
the many generations of our dreams.

and we are the end of his ancient line,
your seed a river of arrested time
whose currents bring the cursed crown
forever back to the foot of this bed —
the double crown of those who wear
the kingdoms of heaven and hell on their head.

the royal bird is blind in morning
and its glamorous wings will shade us
till the end of time. but O my brother
will you wear forever that stolen ring
which wounds your hand by night, and why
in your dreams do you go to the king, the king?

Contents